# GET**STARTED**

## Foundations in English

Nancy Douglas

James R. Morgan

**NATIONAL GEOGRAPHIC**
**L E A R N I N G**

Australia • Brazil • Mexico • Singapore • United Kingdom • United States

## NATIONAL GEOGRAPHIC
### L E A R N I N G

**Get Started Teacher's Guide, Foundations in English**
**James R. Morgan, Author**
**Nancy Douglas, Author**

Publisher: Sherrise Roehr

Executive Editor: Sarah Kenney

Senior Development Editor: Margarita Matte

Assistant Editor: Becky Long

Media Researcher: Leila Hishmeh

Director of Global Marketing: Ian Martin

Senior Product Marketing Manager:
   Caitlin Thomas

Sr. Director, ELT & World Languages:
   Michael Burggren

Production Manager: Daisy Sosa

Content Project Manager: Beth Houston

Senior Print Buyer: Mary Beth Hennebury

Composition: Lumina Datamatics, Inc.

Cover/Text Design: Brenda Carmichael

Art Director: Brenda Carmichael

Cover Image: @Jimmy Chin

Inside Front Cover Image: MIKEY SCHAEFER/
National Geographic Creative

> For product information and technology assistance, contact us at
> **Cengage Learning Customer & Sales Support, cengage.com/contact**
> For permission to use material from this text or product,
> submit all requests online at **cengage.com/permissions**
> Further permissions questions can be emailed to
> **permissionrequest@cengage.com**

Get Started Teacher's Guide ISBN: 978-1-305-94930-0

Get Started Teacher's Guide and Audio CD ISBN: 978-1-337-62118-2

**National Geographic Learning**
20 Channel Center Street
Boston, MA 02210
USA

National Geographic Learning, a Cengage Learning Company, has a mission to bring the world to the classroom and the classroom to life. With our English language programs, students learn about their world by experiencing it. Through our partnerships with National Geographic and TED Talks, they develop the language and skills they need to be successful global citizens and leaders.

Locate your local office at **international.cengage.com/region**

Visit National Geographic Learning online at **NGL.cengage.com/ELT**
Visit our corporate website at **www.cengage.com**

Printed in the United States of America
Print Number: 01   Print Year: 2017

## Acknowledgments

We would like to thank the educators who provided invaluable feedback throughout the development of *Get Started*: Martha Carrasco, Centro de Idiomas Mochis, UAS (Universidad Autonoma de Sinaloa); Catherine Cheetham, Tokai University; Ana Raquel Fiorani Horta, SENAC (Serviço Nacional de Aprendizagem Comercial); Morayma Gomez, Universidad Autónoma de Chihuahua; Solange Lopes Vinagre Costa, SENAC (Serviço Nacional de Aprendizagem Comercial); Deyvis Sanchez, ICDA (Instituto Cultural Domínico-Americano); Ruben Uceta, ICDA (Instituto Cultural Domínico-Americano).

We would also like to thank Raul Billini, English Coordinator, Mi Colegio, Dominican Republic, for his contributions to this series.

## Overview

*Get Started* is a course book for students who have limited to no experience using the English language. Unlike other beginner courses, which often assume a certain base of knowledge, *Get Started* is written for those pre-beginning students who need more language support. After studying with *Get Started*, students will be prepared to move on to a beginning-level course.

## Goals of the course

The goal of *Get Started* is to introduce students to high-frequency, need-to-know language that will enable them to communicate in basic English fluently and with self-confidence. To help learners achieve these goals, *Get Started* provides:

- Topics that relate to students' lives
- High frequency vocabulary and useful expressions
- Clear, accessible grammar models for students to follow
- Numerous opportunities for interactive, meaningful practice with the target language
- Recycling of language throughout the course to help students build a strong, active vocabulary
- Detailed learning goals, ideas for optional classroom activities, and step-by-step support in the Teacher's Guide

## Format

Every six-page unit in *Get Started* is divided into three sections: Vocabulary, Grammar, and Speaking. Each two-page spread provides step-by-step presentation and practice of the target language.

## Support for students

*Get Started...*

- introduces the language of classroom instruction (e.g., *open your book, answer the question*) from the beginning so that students can understand immediately what's happening in the classroom
- relies on visuals rather than written definitions to introduce new vocabulary so students can quickly grasp the meaning

- controls the amount of language input per unit so that students are not overwhelmed by too much content
- offers opportunities for speaking as well as listening so that students develop confidence in using the language
- utilizes different types of communicative tasks (e.g., games, role plays, surveys, and simple presentations) to keep students engaged

## Support for teachers

Support for teachers is enhanced by these special features in the Teachers Guide:

- *Language Notes* supply basic information about words, phrases, and grammar points so that you are well prepared to explain them to your students
- *Prep work* notes give you a heads up on suggested preparations that can be done before teaching a lesson
- *Additional vocabulary* suggestions are provided for vocabulary expansion where appropriate
- The *Challenge* notes provide suggestions on how to make an exercise more difficult for your students while the *Support* notes give suggestions on making an exercise more accessible. These two features allow you to use the materials with students of varying abilities.
- *Expansion* activities provide you with additional ideas for expanding on the language students have already learned
- *Classroom management* tips explain how to adjust the material for larger or smaller classrooms and give time management tips
- *Cultural notes* related to the material are provided where appropriate
- *Pronunciation tips* that provide opportunities for noticing and practicing specific sounds

We have found that working with students at this level, while challenging at times, can be immensely rewarding. We hope that you'll enjoy and learn from working with this material!

Nancy Douglas
James R. Morgan

Pronunciation Tips raise awareness of many of the important features of English sounds. They remind teachers of the complexity of the language. Remember to help students notice the following:

## The vowels system of English

- Five vowel letters can express 15 vowel sounds.

- Sound-spelling correspondence can challenge students whose languages are written almost phonetically.

- All vowels not receiving primary or secondary stress become the "supervowel" /ə/, which constitutes about 75% of all English vowels. Some examples are pencil /ˈpɛnsəl/, common /ˈkɑmən/, focus /ˈfoʷkəs/, animal /ˈænɪməl/, and listen /ˈlɪsən/.

- Vowels can be longer or shorter in extension, depending on if they precede a voiced consonant or a voiceless one. The /æ/ sound in bad /bæd/ is longer than the /æ/ in bat /bæt/.

## Consonants in English

- Many consonants in English are alveolar (/t/ /d/ /n/ /l/ /s/ /z/ /ɾ/) and not articulated behind the front teeth, like in many other languages.

- Consonants also have diverse manifestations that depend on neighboring sounds and stress. For example, the s can be pronounced /s/ after voiceless consonants, like in books /buks/, bats /bæts/, and tips /tɪps/. However, it is /z/ after vowels and voiced consonants, like in pens /pɛnz/, bells /bɛlz/, and mothers /mˆðərz/.

## Suprasegmentals in English

- Intonation needs to be presented early on. Students should learn to notice and produce a rising intonation for *Yes / No* questions versus a rising-falling intonation for questions with interrogative pronouns and affirmative or negative sentences.

  ○ *Yes / No* question.

    Is William at home?↗

  ○ *Wh-* question

    What time is it?↘

  ○ Affirmative / Negative

    I study every day.↘

    I don't like that restaurant.↘

Teachers must also realize that articulatory habits are not internalized in a day, and that providing many opportunities for noticing and practicing the pronunciation of sounds are the key to supporting students. For example, features such as reduction of unstressed vowels to /ə/ are elements that should be worked on in practically every lesson of an introductory level. Perseverance is priceless.

Raul Billini

# SCOPE & SEQUENCE

| | Unit Goals | Vocabulary | Grammar | Listening | Speaking |
|---|---|---|---|---|---|
| **UNIT 1**<br>**CLASSROOM INSTRUCTIONS**<br>p. 2 | Follow classroom instructions;<br>Greet people;<br>Ask someone to repeat | answer, ask, circle, listen, read, say | The imperative:<br>*Open your book.*<br>*Look at the picture.* | Listen to match instructions to actions | *Good morning.*<br>*Can you repeat that?*<br><br>**please, yes / no,**<br>**Numbers 1-5** |
| **UNIT 2**<br>**MY NAME IS ...**<br>p. 8 | Spell names;<br>Meet someone;<br>Say your name | The alphabet | Subject *pronouns: (I, you, he, she);*<br>Simple present:<br>*be*<br><br>**Mr., Ms.** | Listen to spelling of words<br>Listen for contractions | *Hi. I'm...*<br>*It's nice to meet you.*<br><br>**Can you spell that?** |
| **UNIT 3**<br>**OUR CLASSROOM**<br>p. 14 | Identify classroom objects;<br>Ask to use something;<br>Say thank you | backpack, computer, dictionary, pen, phone | Singular and plural nouns;<br>Subject pronouns: *(it, they);*<br>*this / these*<br><br>**ID card** | Listen for contractions | *Can I use your...*<br>*/ Sure.*<br>*Thanks. / You're welcome.*<br><br>**scissors** |

**PUT IT TOGETHER 1**  The Simple Present: *Yes / No* Questions and short answers with *be*; Review of Units 1-3 p. 20

| | Unit Goals | Vocabulary | Grammar | Listening | Speaking |
|---|---|---|---|---|---|
| **UNIT 4**<br>**PERSONAL INFORMATION**<br>p. 24 | Ask for and give personal information;<br>Identify ownership;<br>Talk on the phone | Numbers 1-20 and zero;<br>email address, phone number, student ID number<br><br>**@, .com, .edu** | Subject pronoun: *we;*<br>Possessive adjectives: *my, your, his / her its, our, your, their;*<br><br>**(best) friend** | Listen for email addresses, ID numbers, and telephone numbers | *Excuse me, who's calling?*<br>*Hi, Amy. It's Ray.*<br><br>**different, new, sorry, yeah** |
| **UNIT 5**<br>**MY NEIGHBORHOOD**<br>p. 30 | Talk about places in your neighborhood;<br>Get someone's attention;<br>Ask for and give directions | bank, park, restaurant, school, store<br><br>**favorite** | *There is / There are*<br><br>**street, car, parking garage, tree** | Listen to follow directions on a map | *Excuse me. Is there a / an __ around here?*<br>*Go straight. Turn right / left.*<br><br>**drugstore, library** |
| **UNIT 6**<br>**COUNTRIES**<br>p. 36 | Say countries and nationalities;<br>Ask where someone is from;<br>Describe your city | China / Chinese, Peru / Peruvian Turkey / Turkish<br><br>**flag, language, soup** | *be + adjective;*<br>*be + adjective + noun*<br><br>**interesting, famous, fun, food, actor, beautiful, big/ small, exciting, old** | Listen for countries and nationalities;<br>Listen for sentence stress | *Where are you from?*<br>*I'm from...*<br>*My city is famous for its parks.*<br><br>**near** |

**PUT IT TOGETHER 2**  The Simple Present: *Wh-* Questions with *be*; Review of Units 4-6 p. 42

| | Unit Goals | Vocabulary | Grammar | Listening | Speaking |
|---|---|---|---|---|---|
| **UNIT 7**<br>**FAMILY**<br>p. 46 | Talk about your family;<br>Describe appearance;<br>Ask about age | grandfather, mother (mom), (older / younger) sister, cousin, parents | The Simple Present: *have* (affirmative only)<br><br>*Numbers 21-40, free time, homework, husband* | Listen and identify people in a photo | *You look like your brother / sister.*<br>*How old are you? /*<br>*I'm 21.*<br><br>*on vacation, wife* |
| **UNIT 8**<br>**MY FAVORITES**<br>p. 52 | Describe movies, TV shows and music;<br>Talk about likes and dislikes | funny, popular, scary, hip-hop, pop, rock<br><br>*band / group, singer, song* | The Simple Present: *like* and other verbs (affirmative and negative)<br><br>*play video games, read comic books, watch movies* | Listen for pronunciaiton of verbs ending in -s / -es | *Do you like...?*<br>*Yeah, it's OK.*<br>*No, not really.* |
| **UNIT 9**<br>**TIME**<br>p. 58 | Tell time;<br>Talk about your schedule;<br>Make and reply to a suggestion | art, English, history, math, What time is it? / It's 3:10 | Questions with *when*; Responses with: *at, in, before, after, now, later, today, tomorrow*<br><br>*morning, afternoon, evening, reservation, test, drama club, swim practice* | Listen and complete a class schedule | *Let's study for the test together. / (That) sounds good.*<br>*Are you free in the morning? / No, I have class.* |
| **PUT IT TOGETHER 3**   The Simple Present: *Yes / No* Questions and Short Answers; Review of Units 7-9 p. 64 | | | | | |
| **UNIT 10**<br>**MY ROUTINE**<br>p. 68 | Describe your daily schedule;<br>Explain how often things happen;<br>Talk about your weekend | get up, take a shower, go to school, do homework<br><br>*routine* | Adverbs of frequency<br><br>*choose early late miss (class) nervous* | Listen for how frequently something happens | *What do you usually do on the weekend? / Not much. I…* |
| **UNIT 11**<br>**IMPORTANT DAYS**<br>p. 74 | Say the date;<br>Talk about special days and what people do;<br>Say you know or don't know something | Months of the year (January, February…);<br>Ordinal numbers (first, second…) | The Simple Present: *Wh-* questions with verbs other than *be*<br><br>*What do you do?, check in, buy, serve, wear, have a party, New Year's Day / Eve* | Listen and write the date | *When is the Halloween party? I'm not sure. / I don't know.*<br><br>*film / food festival, last, spring, summer, fall, winter* |
| **UNIT 12**<br>**FOOD**<br>p. 80 | Talk about your favorite foods;<br>Order and pay for food and drinks | *soup and salad, chicken and rice, ice cream, tea*<br><br>*breakfast, lunch, dinner, dessert, eat, drink, milk, soda, water, delicious, good* | Partitives (*a cup of, a slice of*) and *some*<br><br>*healthy, hungry, snack* | Listen to identify foods | *I'd like the chicken sandwich, (please). / Anything else? / A bag of chips, (please). That's $6.50.* |
| **PUT IT TOGETHER 4**   Review of all Question Forms; Review of Units 10-12 p. 86 | | | | | |

Workbook p. 90        Activities p. 102        Vocabulary List p.106

# 1 CLASSROOM INSTRUCTIONS

## 1 VOCABULARY

In this Vocabulary lesson, students will learn to say and understand classroom instructions.

**A** 🔊 Track 2 Listen and repeat.

The verbs introduced in **A** are commonly used in classroom instructions.

Model for students what to do in **A**:

- Look at a picture and point to it.
- Listen to the word said (e.g., *listen*).
- Repeat the word. (Have students say the word.)

Then play the audio and have students do **A**.

### PRONUNCIATION TIP

Remember to model new vocabulary before students see it in written form. Provide two or three model sentences for each word. For example, after you present *open*, demonstrate it by opening a book, a notebook, and a door. Say sentences like, *I open my book in class.*

**EXPANSION** For additional in-class practice with the new vocabulary, do the following:

**PREP WORK** Before class, scan the twelve pictures in **A**, removing the word below each one.

The activity: In class, project the scanned pictures. Point to the pictures and have students call out what each action is. Do this once, allowing students to use their books for reference. After you've gone through all twelve words, tell students to close their books, and then practice again.

**ADDITIONAL VOCABULARY** There are additional instructions that teachers can introduce. Write these on the board and then model them for the class: *raise your hand; stand (up); sit (down).*

Write these on the board and then illustrate their meaning: *match* (a word and a picture); *underline* (the word); *check* (the correct answer).

**B** 🔄 Work with a partner.

1. Cover each row of words on page 2 with a paper.
2. Point to a picture. Use a word in the box.

Model **B** for students

- Direct students to the twelve pictures in **A**. Take a piece of paper and cover the row of words below the first four pictures so that you see only the four images. The goal is to see if students can look at each picture and match it to a word in the box. (The words below the photos will be covered.)

- Point to the first picture. Then direct students' attention to the box with the list of words. Point to the word *listen*. Then point to the picture again and say *listen*.

- Point to the second picture. Ask a student volunteer to tell you the word that goes with it.

- Then put students in pairs. Tell them to take turns doing the same thing with the rest of the pictures, moving the paper down on the page as they complete a row of photos.

**C** 🔄 Work with a partner.

Write the words from **B**.
Put the papers on the desk.

**PREP WORK** Bring extra paper to class so that you can give one or two sheets to each pair of students.

The activity: In class, give each pair a sheet or two of paper. Tell them to do the following:

- Cut the paper into twelve individual pieces. (Model this for students.)

- Write each word in the box in **B** (*answer, ask, circle, …*) on a different paper, as modeled in the first illustration.

- Mix the papers and put them face down in a stack on the desk, as shown in the second illustration. (Model this for students so they understand what to do.)

**D** 👥 Work with another pair. Play the game. Use all the words.

**PREP WORK** Each pair will need paper on which to draw, and a pen or pencil.

The activity: Students are going to play a Pictionary-style game to help them practice the new vocabulary. Each pair should get together with another pair to play the game. Pair 1 will be competing against Pair 2. Model the game once with a student volunteer.

- Starting at the same time, one student from each pair should take a paper from their own stack and read the word on it, as in the illustration on the page. The students should *not* show the words to their partners.

- After reading the word, each student should try to draw a picture of the word for his or her partner. Each student's partner should look at the picture being drawn and try to guess which word from **B** his or her partner is drawing.

**SUPPORT** Allow students to look at **A** to help them guess which word their partner is drawing.

**CHALLENGE** Tell students to close their books. Tell them to try to recall the words being drawn from memory.

- Time students as they do this. They have <u>one minute</u> to draw and guess the word. If the drawer's partner guesses the word correctly, the pair gets one point.

To ensure that students understand the meaning of *correct,* translate the word into students' native language, or use symbols students might know (e.g., ✓ / ✗), or illustrate the words *correct (right)* and *incorrect (wrong)* on the board:

1+1 = 2 (*correct / right*)
1+1 = 4 (*incorrect / wrong*)

- Students should then change roles. Now the students who were drawing watch and try to guess.

- Students should keep playing the game until they use all of the words. At the end, the winner is the pair with the most points.

- For additional practice, have students pair up with a new partner and play the game again.

# 2 GRAMMAR

This Grammar lesson will focus on the imperative. These sentences are all classroom instructions. It will be helpful for students to learn these so that they will be able to understand basic directions in English from the beginning.

**A** 🔊 Track 3 Look at the pictures. Listen and repeat.

- Say each of the words first as students listen. Then say each of the words and have students repeat. Encourage students to pay special attention to the stress of multi-syllabic words.

**EXPANSION** First have students identify which words have more than one syllable. Then as you (and later they) say those words, have them tap out each syllable on their desks, emphasizing the stressed syllable in each word with a louder tap. This is a good way to get students to start becoming aware of word stress from the very beginning.

- Point to different words and have students say each one in unison. Then call on individual students to say the words as you point at them.

**PRONUNCIATION TIP**

Focus students' attention on the /l/ sound in *picture* and *English*. Say the words for them to repeat.

**B** Study the chart.

- Start with the nouns in the chart (*picture, sentence, word,* etc.) that students just learned in **A**. Say them again together.

- Next practice saying the full sentences (e.g., *Look at the picture.*) together. What do the students notice about the words *the, your,* and *and* (the words in red). Explain that some of the sentences use *the* while others use *your* or *and.*

- Now read the words in black while students read the red words. (You: *Read...* Students: *the...* You: *sentence.*) You can also read the first part of each sentence and have students shout out the last word. (You: *Circle the...* Students: *WORD!*) Students can also practice doing this in pairs. Finally, point out the use of *at* and *to* following two of the verbs in the chart: *look at* and listen *to*.

---

**PRONUNCIATION TIP**

The pronunciation of *to* and *at* can be confusing because sometimes they are stressed (/tuː/ and /æt/) and sometimes they are unstressed (/tə/ and /ət/). Some basic rules are: *to* and *at* are stressed at the end of a sentence or question: *I want to*; *What are you looking at?* In general, in other positions *to* and *at* are unstressed: *He's at home*; *I want to go.*

---

**C** 🔊 Track 4 Match the sentences from **B** under the pictures. Listen and check your answers.

- Here is where students will learn the meaning of the sentences in the chart. Have them write each sentence in **B** under the correct picture in **C**. It may be helpful to have students work in pairs to do this activity.

**CLASSROOM MANAGEMENT** To move things along when time is short, give each pair of students only three sentences to write and then have them come together as a class and share their answers. (Note: Multiple pairs can work on the same three sentences.)

- First have students listen and check their answers. You may want to pause the audio after each item to give them time to make any corrections. Once everyone says "OK," proceed.

- For a second listening, have students listen and repeat.

**Answers**
1. answer the question   2. open your book
3. cover the page   4. read the sentence
5. listen to the conversation   6. write your name
7. look at the picture   8. listen and repeat
9. say the word   10. close your book
11. circle the word   12. ask your teacher

**D** 🔁 Work with a partner. Cover **A**—**C**. Write the missing words.

**ADDITIONAL VOCABULARY** This is a good place to teach the word *partner* as it comes up in the direction line here and it will be used repeatedly throughout the book.

- Have students work in pairs. Go over the answers as a class.

- One fun way to go over the answers is to have students count off from 1 to 3. The 1s are the *and* group; the 2s are the *the* group; and the 3s are the *your* group.

- Use the answer that is given in the exercise as a practice round. You say: *Number 1.* Since the answer to that item is *Listen to the conversation*, all the students in the *the* group (Group 2) should stand up. Then you call on one of the students who is standing to read the answer aloud. When you say: *Number 2*, all of the Group 3 students will stand up (because the answer is *Write your name*).

- Since Group 1 (the *and* group) only has one item (*Number 7: Listen and repeat*) you can ask them to read their answer in unison.

- Continue in this way until you've gone through all twelve items in the exercise.

**CHALLENGE** The target verbs and nouns also come in "other combinations." For example, students have learned *Say the word* but you can also say *Circle the word.* To test your students' knowledge, write a sentence and post a simple picture on the board. Then say the following sentences aloud: *Read the word. Circle the sentence. Ask your partner. Cover the word. Say the sentence. Circle the picture.* As you read each one, have students act them out. Can they understand the meaning of these "new" sentences?

**Answers**
1. the   2. your   3. your   4. the   5. the   6. the
7. and   8. the   9. your   10. the   11. the   12. your

---

**PRONUNCIATION TIP**

Point out to students that *the* is pronounced /ðə/ before consonants: /ðə/ word, name, book, and /ðiː/ before vowels: /ðiː/ answer, open door, English book.

---

**E** 🔾 Work in a group. Go to page 102. Play a game. **Student A** says a sentence to **Student B**. **Student B** says a sentence to **Student C**. Say the sentence again, and again. **Student E** says the sentence.

- Put students into small groups of 5–8 students. Have them give themselves letters: A to E for 5 students, A to F for six students, etc.

**CLASSROOM MANAGEMENT** This game works well with groups of five students or more. If you have a small class of 8–9 students, simply put them in one group to play.

- Students are going to play a game called "telephone." Students sit in a circle or a row. The first student will whisper a sentence from page 102 into the ear of the next student. That student will then whisper the sentence into the next student's ear, and so on, until it has been passed down to the last student, who then says the sentence aloud.

- Students have to be careful and whisper so that only the next student in line can hear it. (If other students can hear it, the game won't work.)

- To get each group started, whisper a target sentence in the first student's ear.

**PREP WORK** Another way to play is to prepare the sentences on slips of paper beforehand (one sentence per group of students). When you give the signal, the first student in each group turns over the slip of paper and starts the game.

**CHALLENGE** After students have played a round or two and have the hang of it, you can make the game more difficult by telling them that they can only whisper the sentence in the next student's ear once. If that student misses it, they have to simply continue the game, making their best guess. (This can sometimes result in funny endings to the telephone chain, which is the fun of the game).

**CHALLENGE** Have the different teams compete against each other. The last student in each telephone chain has to race to the board and write the sentence with no spelling errors to win the round.

- If you play several rounds, make sure students shift one seat to the right or left for each successive round so that different students start off in the initial position.

**Answers**
1. answer the question   2. open your book
3. cover the page   4. read the sentence
5. listen to the conversation   6. write your name

7. look at the picture   8. listen and repeat   9. say the word
10. close your book   11. circle the word
12. ask your teacher

# 3 SPEAKING

This Speaking lesson will focus on useful classroom language: numbers 1–5, greetings, and clarification questions.

**A** Say the words and sentences in the Useful Language box with the teacher.

- Point to the box on the page. Say the numbers 1 to 5 and have students repeat them. Then write the numbers 1 to 5 on the board and have students call them out without reading from their books. Do this a few times to give students practice recognizing and saying the numbers in English. Then say *Good morning, Good afternoon, Good evening* and have students repeat. Each expression is a way of greeting, or saying *hello* to others. Make it clear to students when we use each one. You can do this by drawing a clock on the board (or showing the hour on your phone) that says, for example, 9:00 a.m. Point to the clock and say to students, *Good morning.* Do the same with *Good afternoon* and *Good evening.*

**LANGUAGE NOTE** USING GOOD EVENING
*Good evening* is used as a greeting, while *Good night* is used at the end of the evening, when someone is leaving or going to bed.

- Then say the last two expressions (*Can you repeat that? Can you say that again?*) Model with students how we use these questions when we want someone to repeat something.

**PRONUNCIATION TIP**

Point out to students that <u>can</u> is pronounced /kən/ in the affirmative and in questions.

- Look next at the Word Bank. Say the words *yes* and *no.* Model their meaning by moving your head in the appropriate direction, or, if appropriate in your institution, translate the words into students' native language(s).

- Finally, say the word *please* with students. Make sure they understand the meaning of this word and how it's used.

**LANGUAGE NOTE** USING *PLEASE* We often use *please* with directions or commands to make them more polite. The word can come at the beginning or end of these kinds of sentences:

*Please open your books. Open your books, please.*

We also use *please* with requests (to ask for something). For example, in the conversation in **B** the student says, *Can you repeat that?* You can add *please* to this question, though with requests, *please* usually comes at the end of the sentence: *Can your repeat that, please?* (Please can you repeat that?)

**LANGUAGE NOTE** SAYING *GOODBYE* In this Speaking lesson students learn how to greet others at the start of class. When class is over, teach students that they can say the following as they leave: *Bye.* (short for *goodbye*) or *See you.*

**B** 🔊 **Track 5** Read and listen to the conversation.

Point to the photo on the top of the page and have students look at it. Elicit the words *teacher* and *point*, which students have seen in this unit. Then direct students to the dialogue and have them read it. Finally, play the audio once through. For additional practice, play it again and have students repeat each line.

**C** 🔄 Work with a partner. Say the conversation in **B**.

Have students work in pairs to practice the conversation. After they've done it once, have

them changes roles and practice again. If time allows, have students practice again with a different partner.

**EXPANSION** DISAPPEARING DIALOGUE While students are practicing, write the conversation on the board or project it onscreen with some of the words missing, for example:

Teacher: Good _____, everyone. Please _____ your books to page five.

Student: Emily?

Teacher: _____?

Student: Can you _____ that?

Teacher: Yes. _____ to page five.

Tell students to close their books and look at the conversation on the board (or screen). Have them say the conversation again. Can they remember the words? After they finish, erase some more words from the conversation, and have students say it again. Keep doing this until you've erased almost all of the words from the conversation. See how much students are able to remember.

**D** 🔊 **Track 6** Listen. Circle the words.

Tell students to read the two short conversations to themselves. Then have them listen and circle the words and numbers the speakers say.

**E** 🔄 Work with a partner. Say the conversations in **D**.

Have students work with their partner to check their answers in **D** and practice saying each conversation.

**Answers**
1. Teacher: afternoon, 3
   Student: say that again, 3
2. Teacher: morning, 5
   Student: repeat that, 5

**F** Write five actions.

On each line, students should write a different action, like those shown in the examples. These should be actions that students can actually do, using language they've learned on the Vocabulary and Grammar pages. Students will be using these instructions to play a type of "Simon Says" game in **G**.

**G** 👥 Work in a group of four.

1. Say an action from **F**.
2. Students **A–C** do the action.
3. Circle correct (✓) or incorrect (✗) for students 1–3.

- Put students in groups of four. Model **G** for the class with a student volunteer.

- One student in the group starts. The student should say his or her first instruction (e.g., *Close your book.*). The other people in the group (Students 1, 2, 3) should do the action. If they don't understand what the speaker is telling them to do, they can ask the speaker to repeat <u>one</u> time.

- The speaker should then circle in the chart whether each person in the group did the action correctly (✓) or incorrectly (✗). For example, if Action 1 is *Close your book.* and Student 1 does this, under Action 1 he would get a green ✓ for correct. If Student 2 opens his book, under Action 1 he would get a red ✗.

- The student speaking should do the same with all five of his/her commands. At the end, the speaker should give each person in the group his or her score (e.g., *Rosa: five correct, Mario: four correct, one incorrect*).

- Then it's another person's turn.

# 2 MY NAME IS ...

## 1 VOCABULARY

In this Vocabulary lesson, students will learn to say the letters of the alphabet and spell names.

As a lead-in, have students look at the alphabet on the page. Call out ten to twelve different letters and tell students to circle the ones they hear. (Model this once so that students know what to do.) Can students recognize any of the letters when they're said? Check answers with the class.

**A** 🔊 Track 7 **PRONUNCIATION** Listen and repeat.

• Play the audio and have students say each letter after the speaker. If necessary, play the audio a second time for more practice.

• After students have listened to the audio, say the letter *A*. Then point to a student near you and have him or her say the next letter in the alphabet (*B*). The student next to him should then say the next letter (*C*), and so on. Continue around the class having students call out the letters of the alphabet in order until everyone has said a letter.

### PRONUNCIATION TIP

Focus students' attention on the vowel sounds: *a* /eɪ/, *e* /iː/, *i* /aɪ/, *o* /oʊ/, *u* /uː/. Depending on students' native language, *a*, *e*, and *i* may be confusing.

**B** 💬 Work with a partner.

**STUDENT 1:** Say letters A–M.

**STUDENT 2:** Say letters N–Z.

• Tell students to work with a partner. Student 1 should say letters A to M. Student 2 should listen and make sure his or her partner is pronouncing the letters correctly. Then Student 2 should say letters N to Z. Student 1 should make sure his or her partner is pronouncing the letters correctly.

**C** 💬 Repeat **B**. Change roles.

• Student 2 should now say letters *A* to *M*, and Student 1 should say letters *N* to *Z*.

**D** 🔊 Track 8 Look at the picture. Listen to the names 1–5. Write the letters.

• Remind students that they learned the word *name* in Unit 1. Then write the following sentence on the board and complete it with your given name: I'm
_____. (e.g., *I'm Kent.*)
  Name

• Get students to notice that the first letter of a name is always capitalized (e.g., written *K*). Then point to yourself and say the sentence (*I'm…*) using your own name. In the audio, students will hear the people in the photo introduce themselves using this sentence.

• Next, have students look at the photo of the five people. Do number one with the class. Point to the man numbered "1" in the photo. Then play the audio and have students write the letters to complete his name. Then say the name (*Pedro*) and ask for a student volunteer to spell it for the class. Write the answer on the board. Then have students listen and complete the names in 2–5.

**CULTURE NOTE** *NAMES* In many English-speaking countries, people refer to their *first name* and *last name* (i.e., family name or surname), for example: <u>Kent</u> <u>Miller</u>
                                            name   last name

In the example above, *Kent* is the man's first (or *given*) name and *Miller* is his last (or *family*) name. Not every culture follows this pattern. In some Asian countries (e.g., Korea), a person's family name (*Nam*) comes first and the given name (*Hae Jin*) follows. In **D**, each person is saying and spelling his or her first/given name.

In the United States and some other English-speaking countries, it is also common for people to refer to each other by their first name, even if the person is older. This is true among friends, of course. In the workplace, too, colleagues often call each other by their first names, even when speaking to a superior. In some schools, teachers may also tell students to call them by their first names (*Ken, Amelia*). However, in many academic settings, it's best for students to use a title and the person's surname when addressing a teacher (e.g., *Professor Yang, Doctor Price, Mr. Kim, Ms. Nieto*), unless they are told otherwise.

**Answers**
1. Pedro   2. Mahesh   3. Lily   4. Jacob   5. Olivia

**E** ⚡ Work with a partner. Say and spell the names in **D**.

- Say the five names aloud with students, bearing in mind that some may be unfamiliar to your students, or the names may be pronounced differently in students' native languages. As you say the names aloud, focus on the sounds that are challenging for your learners.

- Next, introduce the word *spell* and make sure students understand what to do by spelling answer one (*P-E-D-R-O*) aloud. Then put students in pairs and have them take turns spelling the five names with a partner.

**F** ⚡ Work with a partner. Say and spell your name.

- Have students write their names to complete the sentence: *I'm …* Then they should say and spell their name aloud. If Roman letters are not used in your students' native language, they may need you to help them sound out and spell their names in English. Point out the Notice information. If anyone in the group has a double letter in his or her name, use their name as another example here.

**G** 🎲 Play the game with the class.

1. Write different letters in the chart.
2. The teacher says a letter.
3. Circle the letter in your chart.
4. Circle all your letters to win.
5. Say *Bingo*!

- Tell students to write a different letter of the alphabet in each blank of their Bingo chart. (Every chart in class will be different.) Using this chart, students are now going to play a game of Bingo. Model the first 3 steps below with them.

- The teacher should call out letters at random (or choose them out of a bag).

- When a student hears a letter in his or her chart called, the student should circle the letter.

(The teacher should also remember to note which letter is being called.)

- The first student to circle all the letters in his or her chart and call out *Bingo!* is the winner.

- The winner should read aloud the letters circled in his or her chart; the teacher should check that these were the letters called.

- Play again. This time, have the winner come to the front of the class and call out the letters.

- See page 100 for a printable copy of the Bingo chart you can bring to class for additional practice.

# 2 GRAMMAR

This Grammar lesson will focus on the subject pronouns *I, you, he,* and *she* and introduce students to the simple present of *be* with its three forms: *am, are,* and *is*.

**A** Look at the pictures. Say the words.

- Ask students to look at the pictures. Model the pronunciation of the four subject pronouns as you point to yourself and others. Next, have the students repeat after you as you say each one. Finally, simply point to a person and have the students call out the pronoun.

- Put students into groups of four. Have students take turns saying the pronouns as they point to the appropriate person in their group. (If there is no *he* or *she* in their group, they can point to someone in a neighboring group.)

**LANGUAGE NOTE** Some students mix up *he* and *she*. Keep practicing the pronouns until students feel confident.

**B** Study the chart.

- Students are now going to learn both the full and contracted forms of the four pronouns with the verb *be*.

**LANGUAGE NOTE** A contraction is a short form that comes about by combining two words. Contractions are extremely common in everyday speech and informal writing. A common way of forming a contraction is by replacing a missing letter with an apostrophe ('). There are many different contracted forms in English, but this lesson will focus on the pattern "subject pronoun + *be*" only.

- Have students read the grammar chart silently. Then ask the class for the three verb forms (*am, is, are*). Say the pronouns from **A** again, and have students supply the correct verb form.

**CHALLENGE** Mix up the order of the pronouns to make it more challenging. You can also play a game with the class where you start out slow and gradually speed things up so that students have to supply the verb form very quickly.

- Write the following on the board: *I am = I am = I'm.* Do this for all of the pronoun + verb combinations (*you are / you're; he is / he's; she is / she's*) so that students see how the contracted forms are made. Model the pronunciation of the contracted forms and then contrast the full forms with their contractions.

- Next have the students look at the words in blue. These are the contracted forms. Practice saying the contracted forms and then contrast the full forms with the contracted forms. Finally, practice saying the full sentences in the chart together, *I'm a teacher.* Etc.

---

**PRONUNCIATION TIP**

Note that in the full forms, *is* is pronounced /Iz/. In contractions, the short /I/ is lost: *he's* /hi:z/, and *she's* /ʃi:z/.

---

**C** 🔊 **Track 9** Look at the pictures. Listen and repeat.

- Check to make sure that students understand the additional vocabulary in this exercise: In addition to *student* and *teacher*, they will also learn *soccer player, doctor, businessman/businesswoman,* and *programmer.* Say each profession and have students repeat.

**CHALLENGE** Have students practice spelling some of the shorter words (*student, teacher, doctor*).

- This exercise will give students practice with hearing the contracted forms. Before you play the audio, practice saying the sentences together. To drive home the point that the sentences with contractions have fewer syllables, have students practice saying the sentences to themselves as they tap out the number of syllables on their

desk. This might be a little challenging at first, so demonstrate how to do it with the first pair of sentences. Finally, play the audio and ask students to repeat each sentence.

**LANGUAGE NOTE** When students look at the photo of the *businessman,* introduce the words *man* and *woman* by drawing two pictures on the board. Then ask the students to look at the other photos and identify if each one is a man or a woman.

**D** 🔊 **Track 10** Listen again. Circle the sentences in **C**.

- Play the audio. Students will hear one sentence for each pair. Tell them to circle the sentence that they hear. Go over the answers as a class.

**Answers**
1. I'm a student   2. You're a teacher   3. He is a soccer player   4. She is a doctor   5. He's a businessman
6. She's a programmer

**E** Write the missing words.

- Introduce the abbreviation *Mr.* for a man and *Ms.* for a woman, paying special attention to the pronunciation in the Word Bank. Say them for students to repeat. Explain that both titles are used to describe people who are married or single.

**CULTURE NOTE** *Miss* (for unmarried women) and *Mrs.* (for married women) also describe marital status for women. When you are speaking to a woman from the United States, it's usually best to go with *Ms.* (If the person prefers the title *Mrs.*, she will tell you.) *Miss* can be used in a formal introduction of a young girl, but these days it is not widely used for adult women (though you may hear it used in certain regions).

- Have students read the names/pronouns aloud. At this point, the gender of the subject of the sentence isn't important because the exercise is focusing only on verb forms. Give students time to work. Have them compare answers with a partner before going over the answers as a class.

**Answers**
1. Ms. Yao <u>is</u> a teacher   2. James <u>is</u> a programmer
3. I <u>am</u> a soccer player   4. Mary <u>is</u> a businesswoman
5. You <u>are</u> a student   6. Mr. Lopez <u>is</u> a doctor

**F** Rewrite the sentences from **E**.

- Look back at sentences 1, 2, 4, and 6 in **E**. What gender are each of the people? (Students need to know this information to be able to complete the exercise.) Using your pictures on the board of a man and woman, ask individual students to come to the board and indicate their answers. Another option is to have students raise their right hand if the subject in each sentence in **E** refers to a man and their left hand if it refers to a woman. (Answers: Sentences 1 and 4 refer to women, while sentences 2 and 6 refer to men.)

- Students are now going to rewrite the sentences in **E** by using subject pronouns in their contracted forms. The first answer has been given as a model. (*Ms. Yao* refers to a woman, so students would write the sentence *She's a teacher.*)

- Give the students time to complete the exercise and then go over the answers as a class.

**Answers**
1. She's a teacher    2. He's a programmer
3. I'm a soccer player    4. She's a businesswoman
5. You're a student    6. He's a doctor

**G** ⚡ Write names in the chart. Tell a partner. Say it two ways.

- Students will first work alone and write the name of a soccer player, a teacher, and a businessman or businesswoman in the chart. They can write the names of famous people or of people whom they know in their everyday lives.

- Before they go into pairs, explain to students that they are going to tell a partner about each person in their chart. Point out the language in the speech bubble, which demonstrates what is meant by the instruction to "say it two ways" (i.e., by using the person's name as well as by using the appropriate pronoun contracted with *be*). For example, if a student wrote *Lionel Messi* under "soccer player," they would tell their partner: *Lionel Messi is a soccer player. He's a soccer player.*

**EXPANSION** After each pair has finished, have students rotate and find another partner to work with. To make this into a game, have students score one point for every name in their chart that matches what their partner wrote. In order to do this, ask students to pick the names of famous people. That way they increase the likelihood that they will have a match. For example, if both students in a pair wrote *Lionel Messi,* they each receive a point. The students with the highest point totals after several rotations are the winners.

**H** 👥 Work in a group. Play the game. Take turns.

**SUPPORT** Encourage students to keep a running list of classroom instructions that are used in

English. Each time they encounter a new sentence (such as, *Take turns.*) have them add it to their list.

- Students are going to play a memory game. In this game, they have to say their own name and remember the names of all the students who came before them. As a preliminary step, have students go around the circle / room and say their names (*I'm Celia. I'm Omar.* etc.).

- Then model the game with four students, for example: Celia, Omar, Maya, and Diego. Celia will start the game by saying *I'm Celia.* Next Omar will say *I'm Omar. You're Celia.* The game continues in this way.

- Students need to use the different pronouns they have seen this lesson. When it is Diego's turn, he should say *I'm Diego. You're Maya. He's Omar. She's Celia.* Students use the pronoun *you* for the person who came before them and *he* or *she* for all the other students.

- Keep playing the memory game until someone forgets a name (give them 10–15 seconds to say each sentence) or makes a mistake in pronoun reference or contraction. Start the game over at that point.

**CHALLENGE** After students have played a few rounds, you can make the game more difficult by telling students they have to spell out all of the names (e.g., *I'm Diego. D-I-E-G-O. You're Maya. M-A-Y-A.*)

# 3 SPEAKING

In this Speaking lesson, students will learn to say hello and introduce themselves to others.

**A** Say the sentences in the Useful Language box with the teacher.

- Point to the photo at the top of the page and have students look at it. Elicit the word *businessman.* Explain that the two people are meeting for the first time.

**CULTURE NOTE** The two people in the photo are shaking hands. This is a more formal greeting used in many English-speaking countries when two people meet each other for the first time. In an informal setting, people will often simply nod their head (as if saying *Hi*) when meeting someone for the first time.

- Then point to the Useful Language box and model saying *Hello* and *Hi* with students. Demonstrate the meaning of these words by waving. You can also translate the words into students' native language, if appropriate in your insitution, or have students look up the words in their dictionaries so that they understand the meaning.

---

**PRONUNCIATION TIP**
Model *Hello* carefully so that students perceive that the *e* is /ə/ and the *o* is /oʊ/.

---

**LANGUAGE NOTE** *HI AND HELLO Hi* is more informal than *Hello* and is used commonly in everyday conversation. Students can come to class and greet the teacher and their classmates each day by saying *Hi*.

- Next, model the language used for stating one's name (*I'm … / My name is …*) and have students repeat. Point out that you can say *I'm ….* or *My name is….* (e.g., *I'm Pedro.* or *My name is Pedro.*) The sentences mean the same thing.

- Finally, model saying the expression *It's nice to meet you.* which is used when we meet someone for the first time. You can translate the expression into students' native language, if appropriate, or have students look it up in their dictionaries so that they understand the meaning. Point out that it's common to shorten this to *Nice to meet you.*

**B** 🔊 Track 11 Read and listen to the conversation.

- Have students read the dialogue silently, and then play the audio once through. For additional practice, play it again and have students repeat each line.

**C** 🔁 Work with a partner. Say the conversation in **B**.

- Have students work in pairs to practice the conversation. After they've done it once, have them changes roles and practice again.

**D** 🔁 Work with a partner. Say the conversation. Use your names.

- Have students practice again. This time, they should use their own names in the conversation. Have students change partners and practice the conversation again.

**E** Cover the Useful Language box and the conversation in **B**. Read the conversations below. Guess the words.

- Tell students to cover the Useful Language box and the conversation in **B**, modeling this for them so they know what to do. Then have students look at the first conversation. Do the first line in number 1 with them (*1. A: _____. My name ____ Aya.*) Can they guess any of the words? Then tell students to read the two short conversations to themselves and write their guesses.

**F** 🔊 Track 12 Listen. Write the words in **E**.

- Play the audio. Students should check their answers in **E**, and write the correct words.

**Answers**
1. A: Hi, is   B: Hello, I'm   A: you   B: you
2. A: Hi, I'm   B: Hi, I'm   A: you   B: You

**G** 🔁 Work with a partner. Say the conversations in **E**.

- Have students work with their partner to practice saying each conversation in **E**.

Note: In conversation 2, Paula says at the end *You, too*. Point out to students that *(It's) nice to meet you, too.* can be shortened to *You, too*.

**H** 🔵 Meet six classmates. Write their names below.

- In this activity, students are going to "meet" six of their classmates, using the new language they've learned in this lesson and the unit. Model the activity with a student volunteer. Do the sample dialogue, using your own names. Point out the question in the Word Bank showing how to ask someone to spell a word.

- When students do this activity, they can give their given ("first") name, or they can choose to go by *Mr.* or *Ms.* + *family name* (e.g., *Mr. Yu, Ms. Garcia*). Students should write the name of each person they meet on one of the lines.

**CLASSROOM MANAGEMENT** In smaller classes, encourage students to walk around and meet different people. In a larger class, have students talk to students near them.

**I** 🔁 Work with a partner. Say a sentence about a classmate in **H**. Point to the person.

- Have students pair up with a partner. Using the names in Exercise **H**, they should point to the different classmates they met and say who the person is in a sentence (e.g., *She's Sofia.*) Model this once for students so they know what to do.

**EXPANSION** For additional practice, have students take on a new identity, with a first and last name and an occupation. (This can be a regular name or students can take on the identity of a famous person.) Elicit the jobs students saw in the grammar lesson and write them on the board. Brainstorm a list of five or six more with the class and put these jobs on the board.

- Then have students make five business cards for themselves, each with their "new" full name and occupation on it. Draw or project an example of a business card.

- While students are creating their business cards, put this dialogue on the board or screen.

> A: Hi, I'm ….
>
> B: Hi, …. My name is ….

> A: Can you spell that, please?
>
> B: Yes, it's… (*spell your name*) Here's my card. (*give classmate your business card*)
>
> A: Nice to meet you!

- Review the conversation with students, pointing out the new language (*Here's my card.*) Model the conversation with a student. Then have them repeat **H**, exchanging business cards with the people they meet, looking only at the dialogue on the board when they need help. After a few minutes, erase the dialogue on the board, and see if students can do the exercise without the written support.

- Finally, have students repeat **I**, pointing out the different people they met.

# 3 OUR CLASSROOM

## 1 VOCABULARY

In this Vocabulary lesson, students will identify common objects in a classroom.

**A** 🔊 **Track 13** Look at the pictures. Listen and say the words.

- Have students look at the picture and the title of the unit. Introduce the word *classroom*. Next, have students look at the list of words in the box (*door, whiteboard, clock*). On their own, tell them to find each item on the page. Give them a couple of minutes to do this. Then play the audio. As the speaker says a word, students should repeat it and point to the item on the page.

**B** Write the letters.

- Have students work on their own to write the letters and complete each word.

**CHALLENGE** To make the exercise more challenging, time students. Give them two minutes to complete the ten items.

**LANGUAGE NOTE** *ph* The letter combination *ph* is often pronounced /f/ in English, as in the words *phone* and *alphabet*.

**Answers**
1. pen 2. notebook 3. chair 4. pencil 5. backpack
6. phone 7. dictionary 8. eraser 9. computer 10. table

**C** 🔁 Work with a partner. Say and spell the words in **B**.

- Tell students to work with a partner and to take turns saying and spelling the words in **B**. As students do this, tell them to point to the item on the page (e.g., if a student is spelling the word *pen*, he should point to the pen in the picture).

**EXPANSION** For additional spelling practice, play "Hangman" with the class. Do the following.

- Choose an item from the word list (e.g., *phone*). Do not tell the class.
- On the board, write spaces for each letter in the word (e.g., __ __ __ __ __ ).
- Next to it, draw the "hangman's post":

- Invite students to call out a letter. If the letter is in the word, write it in the correct space on the board. (e.g., __ __ __ *n* __ ).
- If the letter is not in the word, draw a head on the hangman's post. Each time a student calls out an incorrect letter, add another body part (neck, body, an arm, a leg). The goal is for students to guess the secret word and call it out before you draw all body parts. If they do this, they win.
- Play a couple of rounds with the class. Then put students in pairs and have them play using the new vocabulary words.

**D** 🔁 Cover the word list. Look at the picture.

**STUDENT A:** Say the words for a-j.

**STUDENT B:** Say the words for k-t.

- Give students a minute or so to study the photos on pages 14 and 15 again. Then tell students to cover the word list. Student A should point to each item lettered a-j and say what it is. Student

B should check his or her partner's answers. Then Student B should point to each item lettered k-t and say what it is. Student A should check his or her partner's answers.

**E** 🔄 Repeat **D**. Change roles.

- This time, Student A should point to each item lettered k-t and say what it is. Student B should point to each item lettered a-j and say what it is.

**F** Look at the word list. Circle the things in your classroom. Then draw a picture of your classroom.

- Model the exercise for students by pointing to an item in your classroom that is on the word list (e.g., *desk*). Circle this word on the list. What other items on the word list are in the classroom? Have students work on their own to circle the words.

- Then tell them to work on their own to draw a picture of their classroom and the things in it. Students should not label the items with the words, though. Model this for students by drawing an example on the board.

**G** 🔄 Give your picture to a partner. Your partner points to things in the picture and says them.

- Model how to do this using one student's drawing. Point to an item in the student's drawing (e.g., *a chair*), and say what the item is. Then have students work in pairs to do the exercise.

**CHALLENGE** Tell students to close their books. As they point to items in their partner's drawing, see if they can say the words from memory.

**EXPANSION** For more practice, have students get together with a new partner and repeat **G**.

## 2 GRAMMAR

This Grammar lesson will focus on the subject pronouns *it* and *they*, singular and plural nouns, and the use of *this* and *these*.

**A** Look at the pictures. Say the words.

- Ask students to look at the pictures. Model the pronunciation of the two subject pronouns. This is a good time to point out that while *it* refers to objects, *they* can refer to objects or people.

- Point to a person/people or an object and have students practice all of the pronouns that they have learned so far.

  pronouns used to refer to people: *I, you, he, she*
  pronouns used to refer to objects: *it*
  pronouns used to refer to objects or people: *they*

---

**PRONUNCIATION TIP**

*It* is pronounced /ɪt/, the same *i* sound as *is* /ɪz/.

---

**B** Study the chart.

- Elicit the forms of the verb *be* students already know, and the contractions with *I, he,* and *she*. Write them on the board. Students are now going to learn both the full and contracted forms of *it* and *they* with the verb *be*. Give students a moment to study the chart. Focus their attention on the Notice! information. Then ask, what forms of *be* combine with *it* and *they*? (Answers: *it is* and *they are*). Show students how the contracted forms are formed by crossing out the extra letter and substituting an apostrophe. Model the pronunciation of the contracted forms.

- Have students focus their attention on the top half of the chart and the question (*What's this?*). Here is another example of a contraction with the verb *be.* As you point out the illustrations of the pencil and the eraser, explain that this question is used when asking about a single object. To answer the question, point out that we begin the sentence with *It's* and then add a little word (*a*) before the noun that follows: *It's a pencil.* Because the noun *eraser* begins with a vowel sound and it's difficult to say *It's a eraser,* tell students to add the letter *n* to the word *a* so that the sentence can be said smoothly: *It's an eraser.*

- Give students some practice with the structure by asking *What's this?* and pointing at different objects in the classroom. Have the students call out the answers. Then have individual students ask you the question.

**ADDITIONAL VOCABULARY** Since students will only know two words that begin with vowel sounds at this point (*eraser* and *umbrella*), show them (or draw on the board) pictures of three common food words (*apple, egg,* and *orange*) so that students get more practice making sentences with *an* (e.g., *It's an apple.*).

• Next have students study the bottom half of the chart. Again, point out the illustrations and explain that the question *What are these?* is used to ask about *two* or *more* objects. (There is no written contracted form. Point out that for two or more of something, we add the letter *s* to the noun: *pencils.*) Again, go around the room asking the question: *What are these?* while students call out responses. Give the students an opportunity to ask the question as well.

---

**PRONUNCIATION TIP**

Help students notice the difference in the pronunciation of *this* and *these*:

*this* /ðɪs/ (short vowel sound + /s/)

*these* /ðiːz/ (long vowel sound + /z/)

---

**LANGUAGE NOTE** Most plural nouns are formed by adding the letter *s* to the singular form. Although there are exceptions to this rule, it is important to avoid giving students too much information all at once. If necessary, explain that the plural form of *dictionary* is *dictionaries.*

**C** Write the other form.

• This exercise will give students practice in writing contractions and full forms.

**CLASSROOM MANAGEMENT** If you have a smaller class or lots of blackboard space available, have students write their answers on the board so that they can learn from one another. Go over the answers as a class.

**Answers**
1. they're  2. she is  3. it's  4. I am  5. you are
6. he's  7. what is

**D** Track 14 **PRONUNCIATION** Contractions with *is*. Listen and repeat.

• Play the audio. Have students listen and read along the first time and then repeat each sentence aloud the second time.

**E** Track 15 Listen. Circle your answers.

• Before playing the audio, have students read the sentences silently and then aloud. The first time they read each answer (e.g., *It's a map.*) have them point to the object as they say it (provide pictures of any objects not in the classroom).

• Play the audio and have students circle their answers.

**F** Work with a partner. Ask and answer the questions in **E**.

• Have students get into pairs to check their answers and then go over the answers as a class. One way to do this is to have each question and response read aloud by a different pair of students.

**Answers**
1. What is this?  2. It's a bookcase.  3. It is a textbook.
4. What's this?

**G** Write the missing words. Ask your partner the questions.

• Go over the first item with the class. Remind students that because *umbrella* starts with a vowel sound, it is preceded by *an*.

• Students should first work alone and complete the items. (They gradually become more challenging.)

**NOTICE** Tell students that they should use contractions in their answers wherever they can.

• Put students into pairs to check their answers. After that, go over the answers as a class by having six pairs of students (one item per pair) come to the board and write their answers. Watch out for spelling, punctuation, capitalization, and contractions.

**Answers**
1. What's this? It's an umbrella.
2. What are these? They're computers.
3. What are these? They're clocks.
4. What's this? It's a chair.
5. What's this? It's a map.
6. What are these? They're textbooks.

**H** Work with a partner. Correct the sentences together.

• Have students read the four items silently and then give them (in pairs) time to make their corrections. Go over the answers as a class.

**CLASSROOM MANAGEMENT** If necessary, to save time, give each pair a single item and tell them that they have a minute to make their correction. (Some pairs will be working on the same item.) After the minute has passed, go over the answers together as a class.

**Answers**
1. What are these? They're notebooks.
2. What's this? It's an ID card.
3. What are these? They're notebooks.
4. What's this? It's a phone.

**I** 👥 Work in groups of four. Play the game.

**STUDENT A:** Show an item or items from your backpack. Ask, What's this?/ What are these?

**STUDENT B-D:** Say the item(s). Correct answer = 1 point.

- Have students form groups of four. The first student (Student A) should take an item out of his or her backpack, book bag, or purse and ask *What's this?* The students should answer *It's a ___*. Rotate so that each student has a chance to be Student A.

- After concluding that practice round, start the game. Student A asks *What's this?* or *What are these?* (depending on the item) and then produces the item from their bag/backpack. The other students try to guess the item. For each correct answer (full sentence) the student receives a point. Play one or two rounds of the game, encouraging students to use both singular and plural nouns.

- To have enough items for students to play the game, you may need to preteach some additional vocabulary, such as *keys, glasses, headphones, earphones, wallet,* or *highlighter.*

**NOTICE** Remember, you have to be able to count the noun for it to work in this game. Nouns such as *makeup* (noncount) won't do.

**CLASSROOM MANAGEMENT** For a quieter version of this activity, have students work in pairs and take turns asking each other the questions.

# 3 SPEAKING

In this Speaking lesson, students practice asking to use something as well as saying *thank you* and replying.

**A** Say the sentences in the Useful Language box with the teacher.

- Direct students' attention to the Useful Language box. Model asking the question by pretending that you need a pen. Go over to a student who has one, point to it, and say *Can I use your pen?* When the student hands it to you, encourage him or her to say *Sure.* Point out that *sure* is a way

to say *yes* when someone asks for something. Then say the question (*Can I use your pen?*) and the reply (*Sure.*) again and have students repeat after you.

- Finally, say the expressions for giving and replying to thanks. Have students repeat. If appropriate in your institution, translate these into students' native language or have students look up the expressions in their dictionary so that they understand the meaning. Point out that *Thank you* and the reply *You're welcome* are more formal than *Thanks* and the reply *No problem.*

**B** 🔊 Track 16 Read and listen to the conversation.

- Have students read the dialogue and then play the audio once through. For additional practice, play it again and have students repeat each line.

**C** 🔄 Say the conversation in **B**.

- Have students work in pairs to practice the conversation. After they've done it once, have them changes roles and practice again. Encourage students to ask each other for different objects (e.g. *eraser, pencil, dictionary*).

**D** Cover the Useful Language box and the conversation in **B**. Read the conversations below. Guess the words.

- Tell students to cover the Useful Language box and the conversation in **B**, modeling this for them so they know what to do. Then tell students to look at the first conversation. Can they guess any of the words? Have students read the two short conversations to themselves and write their answers.

**E** 🔊 Track 17 Listen. Write the words in **D**.

- Play the audio. Students should check their answers in **D**, and write the correct words or part of a word.

**Answers**
A: thank, re
B: Thanks, No

**F** 🔄 Say the conversations in **D**.
Have students work with their partner to practice saying each conversation in **D**.

**G** 🔄 Look at the pictures. Ask and answer the questions.

Start by calling students' attention to the Word Bank note about *scissors*. Say the word with students and point out that this word is always plural. Model the activity by pointing to a picture and asking a student, *What's this?*, and then *What are these?* Then have students work with a partner and take turns pointing to each photo and asking what it is. Tell students to answer in complete sentences. Monitor students to ensure that they're using the correct language.

**Answers**

It's an eraser. It's a phone. It's a dictionary. They're scissors. They're (colored) pencils. It's an umbrella.

**H** 🔁 Say the conversation in **B** again.

- Use a word from **G** in the question.

- Thank and reply to each other.

- Have students say the conversation in **B** again, this time using items from **G**. When students have the conversation, encourage them to give their partner an item if they have it (e.g., if a person asks, *Can I use your eraser?* The other student should give him or her the eraser.) Remind students to thank each other. Also, encourage them to try doing the dialogues without reading from **B**.

**I** 🔁 Repeat **H** with a new partner.

- Assign students to different partners and have them ask to use things.

**EXPANSION** For more practice with *It's a…, They're…,* and thanking people, have students play this gift exchange game.

- Write the word *gift* on the board, and make sure students understand its meaning. (You can show a photo of a gift or have students look the word up in their dictionaries.)

- Then tell students to take a small slip of paper. On it, they should write the name of a gift, or to make it more challenging, draw only a picture of it. The gift can be something simple (like a book or a phone), or it can be something silly (like an eraser) or something expensive (like a car). Encourage students to use words learned in this unit, but also help them with any new words they want to use and put this vocabulary on the board. Once students have written (or drawn) their gift, they should fold the slip of paper in half.

- Next, put students in small groups and tell them to sit in a circle. One student should begin by giving his "gift" to the person on his right. (Model this once for students so they know what to do.) That person should "open the gift" by reading what's on the paper (or trying to figure out what's been drawn), and saying aloud to the group what the item is (e.g., *It's a book!*). The person receiving the gift should then thank the person who gave it to him (e.g., by saying, *Thanks, Mario!*), and the gift giver should reply (*You're welcome.* or *No problem!*). Again, model this for students so they know what to do.

- At the end, have the group vote on the best gift and tell the class.

# PUT IT TOGETHER

## 1 GRAMMAR

> This Grammar lesson will introduce *Yes / No* questions with *be* and short answers (*Are you a student? Yes, I am. / No, I'm not.*).

**A** Study the chart.

- Before introducing the question form, it's a good idea to review statement word order. First elicit the subject pronouns from students (*I, you, he, she, it, they*) and write them on the board. Then have students come up with a sentence for each pronoun that they have learned and put it on the board. (e.g., *I'm a student. You're a teacher.*) Students should use contractions and check the sentences to make sure they are using the correct form of the verb *be*. Leave these sentences on the board.

- Explain to students that they are now going to learn how to ask questions in English. Look at the chart. Read the statements together. Then go over the statements one by one and read the corresponding question for each one. What do they notice about the question forms? (Answer: The appropriate form of the verb *be* comes before the subject in questions. The two words switch places, in a sense. Also, statements end with a period while questions end with a question mark.)

- Now go back to the statements on the board and work with each one to turn it into a question.

**SUPPORT** If it is helpful, first change all of the contractions to their full forms before turning them into questions: *I'm a student → I am a student → Am I student?*

- Practice reading the questions together with rising intonation.

**B** Write questions.

- Because of the prep work you've done in **A** it should be clear to students how to complete the items in **B**. Go over the first example and then give students time to write out their questions for the remaining items. Go over the answers as a class.

  **Answers**
  1. Am I in this class? 2. Are you a teacher? 3. Is he a teacher? 4. Is she a programmer? 5. Is it an eraser? 6. Are they at home?

**C** Follow the pattern. Write statements and questions.

- For this exercise, students will be using the words in the chart to form both statements and *yes / no* questions. Some students may not have seen this exercise type before, so take the time to explain to them how it works. The best way to do this is by working through the first item together.

- In item number 1, the letters B, C, D, and E correspond to the columns in B, C, D, and E in the chart above. Students should choose one word from each of those four columns and construct a grammatically correct sentence (which could be a statement or a question). The challenge comes from the fact that the words are mixed up so students will have to figure out which ones to use. In this case, the answer is *He is a student*, which students can see in their books. Point out the use of appropriate capitalization and punctuation at the end of the sentence.

- Moving on to item number 2, students should then choose one word each from columns B, C, D, E, and F to make a sentence.

**SUPPORT** What makes this engaging for students is that they don't know what kind of sentence to make (statement or question) so they really have to concentrate. If necessary, tell them that items 1–3 are statements and 4–6 are questions.

**CHALLENGE** You can turn this into a game. Put students into groups of four. Two students (A and B) will stay in their seats while the other two (C and D) will be stationed at the board. At the count of three, the game will begin. A and B will look at item 2 and figure out the answer. Once they think they know the answer, they should raise their hands. Student C should then rush over to them, listen to them whisper the answer, and then return to the board to tell D, who will write the sentence on the board. Students should work through all of the items and the first team to have their sentences on the board, spelled and punctuated correctly, are the winners. The key in this game is that students cannot speak, except to whisper the answer to each other.

**Answers**
1. He is a student.   2. He is an English teacher.
3. They are students.   4. Is he a student?
5. Is he an English teacher?   6. Are they students?

**D** 🔊 Track 18 Listen. Write the missing words.

- Go over the expression *I don't know* in the Word Bank. Students will hear it in this listening exercise, but it is also an extremely useful expression for them to know.

- Have students read through the items and guess the missing words. Then play the audio and have them write their answers. Review the answers as a class. Make sure students remember *a/an* in their answers. Have students practice reading the sentences aloud.

**Answers**
**Conversation 1:** What's this? / I don't know. Is it a laptop?
**Conversation 2:** Is she an English teacher? / I don't know. Maybe.
**Conversation 3:** What are these? / I don't know. Are they maps?

**E** Study the chart.

- Students have had the opportunity to practice using *Yes / No* questions. Now they are going to learn how to respond to them with short answers. (They're called "short answer" because it is not necessary to repeat the information in the question when you respond: *Are you a student? / Yes, I am ~~a student~~.*)

- Read through the questions on the left. First have students listen and repeat. Then have students say the questions themselves. Listen for rising intonation when students say their questions.

**LANGUAGE NOTE** The first thing for students to notice in short answers is the pronoun "shift"

that occurs. For example, the question *Are you a student?* elicits the answer *Yes, I am.* This is important to be aware of as it will come up in the exercise that follows. Students should also notice how contractions are used. (Answer: They are used in negative responses but not in affirmative ones.) The contracted form presented in this lesson is pronoun + *be* contraction followed by *not*, as in *you're not, she's not,* etc.

**NOTICE** If any students are familiar with the other contracted form of pronoun followed by *be + not* contraction as in *you aren't, she isn't,* etc., tell them it is correct but to focus on the form in this lesson for now to avoid confusion.

- Ask individual students *Yes / No* questions in order to elicit short answers. (Mix these up to make it challenging for students.)

  *Are you a teacher?*
  *Are you a student?   Am I a teacher?*
  *Am I a soccer player?   Is her nickname Lisa?*
  *Is his name Flavio?   Are they in class?*
  *Are they at home?*

**F** Read the questions. Circle the answers.

- Read through the questions together. Make sure students understand the information in the Notice! box.

- Students should then circle the correct response for each one. Have students compare their answers with a partner and then go over the answers as a class.

**Answers**
1.b   2.b   3.a   4.b   5.a   6.b

**G** Look at the pictures. Write the missing words.

- Ask students to look at the pictures and write in the missing words to complete the questions and short answers. Go over the answers as a class, then have students get into pairs and take turns asking and answering the questions.

**EXPANSION** Have students come up with their own questions (either on the spot or they can write them down ahead of time) and put them in pairs to take turns asking and answering the questions. They should use the four questions in this exercise as a model and come up with one question each using the pronouns *it, they, he,* and *she*.

**Answers**
1. Is <u>it</u> a backpack? / Yes, <u>it</u> is.   2. <u>Are they</u> phones? / No, <u>they're not</u>.   3. <u>Is he</u> a businessman? / No, <u>he's not</u>.
4. <u>Is she</u> a soccer player? / <u>Yes, she is</u>.

**EXPANSION** Have students get into groups of 5–8 students. Introduce the word *nickname,* and then have them write their own nickname on a scrap of paper. It can be a current nickname or a nickname they had when they were little. Also, they can make up a nickname if they don't currently have one. The important thing is that no one else sees what they are writing.

- Shuffle the scraps of paper and put them into a pile. Have one student take the first piece of paper and read the nickname (e.g., *Kike*). He/She should choose one other student and ask *Is your nickname Kike?* The student should answer with the appropriate (i.e., truthful) short answer.

- If the answer is *yes* the questioner gets a point for guessing correctly and the next student will draw a piece of paper, read the nickname, and try to guess who it belongs to by asking *Is your nickname…?* If the answer is *no* the questioner doesn't receive any points and the next student will continue the game by asking the question to another student in order to find out who Kike is.

**CLASSROOM MANAGEMENT** The game works better with larger groups, but if you have a smaller class, simply play this game as one large group.

**EXPANSION** After students have played a round, assign a letter to each student in the group (e.g., if you have six students per group, each student would be assigned a letter from A through F.). Tell all the As, Bs, Cs, and so on, to get together and form new groups and play the game of guessing nicknames again. This time they should ask the question *Are you (Kike)* in order to elicit a response using different pronouns (i.e., *Yes, I am* or *No, I'm not*).

# 2 SEE IT AND SAY IT

**A** Look at the picture. Find the 15 (fifteen) people and things. Write the words.

- In this exercise, the items in the picture are not numbered or labeled. It is up to the students to find and identify as many objects/people as possible.

- There are many different ways to do this activity:
  1. Go around the class and have one student at a time identify an item in the picture. Then ask

everyone to write it down. As the exercise proceeds, it will become more challenging.

2. Put students into pairs (A and B). Divide the drawing in half. The A students should find the items on one half of the drawing while the B students find the items on the other half. The A and B students should then come together and share their lists with each other.

3. Students can work in pairs and race against the clock to find all of the items.

4. Put students into groups of four. The first student in each group will write one item on the list and then pass the book around for another student to add another item and so on, until the list is complete.

- Check to make sure everyone has all 15 items. Take a poll: Which ones were hardest to remember in English?

**Answers**
programmer, businessman, phone, (laptop) computer, pen(s), notebook, chair(s), clock, bookcase, umbrella(s), table, desk(s), door, screen, window.

**B** 🔁 Work with a partner. Point to something in the picture. Ask questions about things. Practice spelling. Take turns.

- In this activity, students will practice spelling. This will be a good way to catch any errors that have crept in when students were creating their lists in **A**.

- Put students into pairs and have them take turns asking their partner about an item in the picture using the dialogue on the page as a model. Practice first as a class with both singular (*What's this / It's a clock*) and plural (*What are these / They're computers*) so that students are prepared for both forms.

# 3 LISTENING

**A** Read the conversations. Guess the answers.

- Ask students to look at the pictures and read the conversations. Have them guess the answers before they listen based on the context.

**B** 🔊 Track 19 Listen. Check your answers in **A**.

- Play the audio for students to check their answers.

**C** 🔁 Cover the conversations in **A**. Choose a picture. Write your own conversation.

- Put students into pairs. Have them cover the dialogues but tell them they can use the photos to remind them of the context for each conversation. Each pair should choose one of the pictures and write a conversation so that each person is speaking at least twice. (Encourage students to write longer conversations too.)

- Circulate around the room, assisting as necessary. Allow students time to practice their conversation.

**D** ⚅ Say your conversation for another pair.

- Once the conversations are written, each pair of students should join another pair and read their conversations for each other. After one round of that, encourage students to perform their dialogues, this time by reading from their papers as little as possible. If time allows, have pairs choose a different picture and repeat **C** and **D** for more practice.

# 4 CROSSWORD PUZZLE

**A** Complete the puzzle. Go to page 103.

- Illustrate the meaning of the words *down* (↓) and *across* (→) by writing them on the board with arrows. Then direct students to sentence 1 (down) and read it aloud (*Listen to the ____.*). Have students look at the number of spaces there are for the missing word. Can they guess what it is? Tell students to write a letter in each blank to complete the word.

**SUPPORT** If students are struggling, write or say the first three letters of the word (*c-o-n*), and see if they can finish it. If they can't, add two more letters.

- Then look at sentence 3 (across), read it aloud, and see if students can guess the missing word. This time, they'll have some help because one letter (*o*) will already be filled in.

- Have students work on their own to complete the puzzle. Then have them check answers with a partner by saying each sentence aloud and spelling the missing word (e.g., *Listen to the conversation. C-O-N-V-E-R-S-A-T-I-O-N*). Review answers as a class.

**SUPPORT** Have students work together in pairs to complete the puzzle.

**CHALLENGE** Have students (individually or in pairs) race against each other to be the first to complete the puzzle. The first person (or pair) to finish should stand up. This student (or pair of students) then has to say each sentence aloud and spell the missing words.

# 4  PERSONAL INFORMATION

## 1  VOCABULARY

In this Vocabulary lesson, students will learn to say numbers zero through twenty and to *ask for* and *give* their phone number and email address.

**A** 🔊 **Track 20**  Listen. Say the numbers.

- Warm up: Review saying numbers 1–5, which students learned in Unit 1. Write the five numbers on the board. Then point to different numbers and with books closed, have students call out the word for each one. Do this a few times. Then have students open their books and direct their attention to the numbers on the page. Play the audio. As the speaker says a number, have students repeat it. Do this a second or third time so that students get practice hearing and pronouncing the numbers.

**EXPANSION**  Put students in pairs. Write on the board:

Student A: Say numbers 0–10.
Student B: Say numbers 11–20.

- As Student A says numbers 0–10, Student B should listen and make sure his or her partner is saying the numbers correctly. Then Student B should say numbers 11–20, and Student A should listen and make sure his or her partner is saying the numbers correctly.

- Then have students repeat the exercise. As they say their numbers, they should do so with books closed.

- Finally, have students change roles. This time, Student B should say numbers 0–10, and Student A should say numbers 11–20. Have them practice with books open and then closed.

**EXPANSION**  Have students create flashcards for the numbers 0–20. On each card (or slip of paper), they should write a number on the front (e.g., *14*) and the corresponding word on the back (e.g., *fourteen*). Have students mix up their cards and then quiz each other. Flashcards are a learning aid that students can create and use to practice and review vocabulary in this unit and all others in the course.

**EXPANSION**  Play a game of Bingo. See page 100 for a printable copy of the Bingo chart. Print enough of these so that each student can play multiple games.

- Give a blank Bingo chart to each student. Tell students to write a different number in each space of their chart. (Every chart in class will be different.) Then model the first 3 steps below with them.

- Call out numbers zero through twenty at random (or choose them out of a bag).

- When a student hears a number in his or her chart called, the student should circle the number. (You should also keep track of which numbers have been called.)

- The first student to circle all the numbers in his or her chart and call out *Bingo!* is the winner. *Variation:* The first student to get a row of numbers vertically or horizontally wins.

- The winner should read aloud the numbers circled in his or her chart while you confirm that these were the numbers called.

- Play again. This time, have the winner call out the numbers.

**B** 🔄  Work with a partner. Circle the words (*zero, one, two*...) in the puzzle.

- Put students in pairs and see how quickly they can find the words in the chart. Note: The words in the puzzle only go vertically & horizontally, not backwards or diagonally. Find one or two of the words horizontally or vertically together to get students started.

**CHALLENGE** Have one pair play against another to see who can locate all the words fastest.

**CLASSROOM MANAGEMENT** If time is short, play this as an elimination game. Give students one or two random words to find and have them stand up after they have found the words. The first 5–10 students who are successful go through to the next round. For each successive round, eliminate one or more students until you have a winner.

**Answer**

| G | C | S | I | X | T | E | E | N | T | E | N |
|---|---|---|---|---|---|---|---|---|---|---|---|
| C | T | H | I | R | T | E | E | N | I | N | E |
| S | J | F | S | E | V | E | N | T | E | E | N |
| E | T | I | Z | I | F | U | S | E | V | E | N |
| I | W | V | E | K | O | L | I | A | O | N | E |
| G | E | E | R | F | U | H | E | F | Z | G | J |
| H | L | F | O | U | R | T | L | I | G | N | T |
| T | V | S | E | R | T | W | E | F | H | R | H |
| E | E | R | S | O | E | O | V | T | X | G | R |
| E | N | N | I | N | E | T | E | E | N | H | E |
| N | L | G | X | R | N | T | N | E | L | X | E |
| Y | E | I | G | H | T | W | E | N | T | Y | W |

**C** 🔊 **Track 21** Look at the chart. Listen to Dmitry.

- Direct students' attention to the class list. Preview the categories in the chart (*student ID number, email address, phone number*), and make sure that students understand what each one means. To illustrate the meaning of *email address*, write an example of a common one used in your country. Do the same with an example phone number.

- Next, have students look at the Word Bank. Point out that the items introduced here are all used to say an email address. Say the words aloud and have students repeat.

**PRONUNCIATION TIP**

The words *dot* and *com* are pronounced with /ɑː/, /dɑːt/ /kɑːm/.

- Then tell students to look at the information in the chart about Dmitry. Play the audio and have students follow along. When Dmitry is done, draw students' attention to the Notice! note and have

them read it. Point out that when Dmitry gave his student ID number, he said *zero seven*… But when he gave his phone number, he used *oh* and not *zero (two nine oh…)*. In American English, it's common to say *oh* (not *zero*) when giving a phone number.

**CULTURE NOTE** PHONE NUMBERS In the United States, phone numbers have ten digits and are written like this: (408) 615–2739. The three-digit area code (shown in parentheses) is followed by a seven-digit phone number. Phone numbers are usually said digit by digit as follows: four oh eight / six one five / two seven three nine. Here, the area codes are not included in the listening exercise.

**D** 🔊 **Track 22** Listen. Complete the chart in **C**.

- Before students listen, have them look quickly at the other three students' information in the chart so that they're familiar with it. Then play the audio and have students write the numbers and email extensions (.com, .net) that they hear. Play the audio a second or third time as needed.

**Answers**
Amelia Ortiz: 04-18-14, Amelia11@linkmail.com, 304-7914
Max Tran: 06-15-10, Max19@starlink.net, 615-6807
Leah Yu: 08-11-17, LeahYu@ CCF.edu, 505-7712

**E** 🔊 Work with a partner.

- Point to a student in **C**.

- Say the information.

- Put students in pairs and have them take turns checking their answers in **C** by pointing to a person and saying his or her name and information. After students have done this, check answers as a class. Write the names from the chart in **C** on the board (*Amelia, Max, Leah*). Then ask a student volunteer to go to the board. Have another student call out *Amelia's* information while the student at the board writes it. With help from the class, make corrections as needed. Then ask another student volunteer to go to the board and have a different student call out *Max's* information. Do the same with *Leah's*.

**EXPANSION** Make a list of random phone numbers with area codes (e.g., (510) 711-8042) or do a search for important phone numbers students might need. Then dictate these to the class and have students write the numbers. Do the same with email addresses.

**F** Write your email address and phone number.

- For this exercise, students can use their real email address and phone number or they can make one up.

**G** 🔗 Ask five classmates for an email address and phone number. Write the information in your notebook.

- Direct students' attention to the speech bubbles. Point out how to ask and answer the question:

  **What's your** email address? **What's your** phone number?
  **It's**... **It's**...

- Then model the exercise by working with a student volunteer. Write his or her name on the board. Then ask for his or her email address and phone number. Write the information on the board next to the student's name. After you've written both, ask the student: *Is the information correct?*

- When students do the exercise, tell them to write each person's name, phone number, and email address in their notebook (as in the model on the board). After they've written a person's information, they should ask the person to check that the phone number and email address are correct.

**SUPPORT** Write on the board, *Can you...?* and elicit the questions: *Can you repeat that? Can you spell that?* Write them on the board. As students are doing the exercise, remind them that they can use these expressions, which they've already learned in earlier units.

**CLASSROOM MANAGEMENT** Instead of having students walk around and interview each other at random, form two lines (line 1 and line 2) each with five students. (In larger classes, you can have multiple pairs of lines.) The students in the two lines should face each other. Tell students to start, and students should take turns asking for the phone number and email address of the person opposite them. Time students as they do this. When time is up, signal for the students in line 1 to shift down a space. (The person at the end of line 1 should then move to the front of the line.) Now students should ask for their new partner's email address and phone number. Continue in this way until students speak to five different people.

# 2 GRAMMAR

This Grammar lesson will focus on possessive adjectives (*my, your, its, our,* etc.). It will also introduce *we* as well as review the subject pronouns that students have already learned.

**A** Study the chart.

- Before you get to the chart, ask one student to stand and say *You are a student*. Next have two or three students stand, look at them and say *You are students*. (This is to introduce students to both the singular and plural forms of *you*.) As the students remain standing, tell the whole class *They are students*. Finally, write the sentence *We are students* on the board and have one of the students who is standing say it aloud. Check to make certain that everyone understands the meaning and usage of plural *you* and *we* before moving on.

- Ask students to look at the left two columns of the chart. Have them practice the subject pronouns and example sentences by repeating after you and by saying it on their own. Ask individual students to make different sentences using the subject pronouns in the chart (e.g., *I'm a student / You're a teacher / It's a table*).

- Next introduce students to the information on possessive adjectives in the right two columns of the chart.

**LANGUAGE NOTE** Possessive adjectives come before nouns. They show ownership or who the noun "belongs to." *This is <u>my</u> pen. It belongs to me.*

- Read through the possessive adjectives and example sentences together as a class. Point out that possessive adjectives are always followed by another word, such as *name* or *teacher*. Also point out that while subject pronouns use apostrophes (when they are contracted with *am, is,* or *are*) possessive adjectives don't.

**NOTICE** 1. Make sure students are clear on the difference between *its* (possessive pronoun) and *it's* (contracted form of *it is*). 2. Watch for spelling errors in the use of *your* and *their* (possessive adjectives) and *you're* and *they're* (contracted form of *you / they are*). 3. Some students may want to erroneously add an *–s* to a possessive adjective such as *our* to "make it plural" (e.g., ~~ours~~). Keep an eye out for that and correct any errors as they arise.

**EXPANSION** Have students say and respond to sentences using possessive adjectives. For example, if one student says *My name is Maria* the next student can say *Your name is Maria* while a third says *Her name is Maria*. You can do this with other sentences in the chart as well.

**B** Cover the chart in **A**. Match the words.

- First look at the picture and read the sentences together. Tell students that the two sentences are two ways of saying the same thing. One shows the usage of the subject pronoun + *be* (*I'm*) while the other shows the possessive adjective (*my*).

- Have students cover the chart in **A** with a piece of paper and work silently to match the subject pronouns to their corresponding possessive adjectives. Go over the answers together as a class and answer any questions the students may have. Note that the singular and plural forms of *you* on the left both match to the word *your* on the right.

**Answers**
| | | |
|---|---|---|
| 1. c | 2. a | 3. f |
| 4. g | 5. b | 6. e |
| 7. a | 8. d | |

**C** Underline the words that are blue in **A**.

- This exercise gives students practice identifying possessive adjectives in a sentence.

- First, go over the example together. Then have them work alone or in pairs to do the remaining items.

**CHALLENGE** 1. Have students cover **A** and **B** with a piece of paper while they are doing **C**.

2. In addition to having students underline the possessive adjectives, ask them to circle the subject pronouns as well. Note: Not all of the sentences have them. (Answers: 1. She   4. I   6. he   9. They)

- Go over the answers together as a class and practice reading the sentences as well.

**Answers**
1. our   2. His   3. Your   4. my   5. your   6. your   7. her
8. Their   9. my   10. Its

**D** Write the missing words.

- Have students look at the first picture and go over the example together. Then complete 3 with the class.

- Before students start the exercise, explain that they should use contracted forms (*I'm, you're* etc.) wherever possible. For example, the answer to item 4 would be *He's a programmer*. Give students time to complete the exercise and compare with a partner, then go over the answers as a class.

**CLASSROOM MANAGEMENT** If time is short, put the class in pairs and have each pair work on the items below only one of the photos.

**Answers**
1. <u>Her</u> name is Clara   2. <u>She's</u> a student
3. <u>Her</u> email address is clara.ar@zmail.com
4.<u>He's</u> a programmer.
5. <u>His</u> phone number <u>is</u> 555-1212   6. <u>His</u> <u>name</u> is Justin.
7. <u>They're</u> a family   8. <u>Their</u> last name <u>is</u> Soams
9. Emily Soams is 20. <u>She's</u> my best friend
10. <u>We're</u> students   11. <u>Our</u> class <u>is</u> in Room 5.

**E** Think of a person. Write the information.

- Give students time to think of someone they know. Preferably it should be someone whom they know well enough to be able to complete the chart (with the person's first and last name as well as phone number and email address). If they have a particular person in mind, but don't know some of the information, it's OK if they just make it up.

- As students are filling in their charts, circulate and check for spelling.

**F** 🔁 Tell a partner.

- Students will now get practice with the possessive adjectives as they tell their partner about the person whom they wrote about in their chart.

**EXPANSION** 1. Students can do the activity in pairs and then pair up with a different partner to tell them about the first partner's person. 2. Have students do **E** and **F** again, but this time they should write about themselves and one other person (e.g., a sibling or a friend). When they tell a partner, they should be careful to use the appropriate forms (e.g., _Our first names are Pablo_ and _Maria. Our last name is Sanchez. My phone number is…. Her phone number is…_ )

**G** 🎲 Get into small groups. Play the game.

- Students are going to play a guessing game in groups of 4–6 students. One student (Student A) will begin by turning around while the remaining students (B-D) retrieve different personal items from their backpacks and purses. It's important that Student A not be able to see this process.

- Student A then turns around and tries to guess who each item belongs to. Encourage the student to use different possessive adjectives (such as _her_ or _his_) so that all of the sentences don't use _your_.

- One way to score the game is to have each student put two objects on the table. The winner is the person who can guess all the items correctly with the fewest number of sentences. Play several rounds so that each student gets at least one opportunity at guessing.

**SUPPORT** Before you start the game, review the vocabulary for everyday objects with students and remind them that _this is_ is used with singular objects (like _book_ and _pen_) while _these are_ is used with plural objects (like _glasses_ and _notebooks_). Also, before each student begins to guess, circulate around the room and make sure that students know how to name all the items on the table.

**CLASSROOM MANAGEMENT** If you have a smaller class, you can play the game with one group of 10–12 students. Also, another way to play with a larger group is to have a group of 10 or more students place objects on the table while a team of 3–4 students take turns guessing. Each student gets one guess. A correct guess means that you get to go again. An incorrect guess means your turn is over. The students who guesses the most items correctly at the end of the round is the winner.

# 3 SPEAKING

In this Speaking lesson, students will practice answering the phone and identifying themselves.

**A** Say the words and sentences in the Useful Language box with the teacher.

- Have students look at the photo of the man talking on the phone. Get students to think about what they say in their own language when they answer the phone (e.g., _Diga? Yeoboseyo?_). Then, direct students' attention to the Useful Language box. Model saying _Hello?_ and have students repeat. Point out that the caller (the person making the call) would reply by identifying himself and saying _Hi…, It's…_ (e.g., _Hi, Mario. It's David_.) Role play this once with a student volunteer. Pretend to call the student. He or she should answer and say _Hello?_. Then you should identify yourself by saying _Hi, Susan. It's…_

**LANGUAGE NOTE** When we identify ourselves, we normally use _I'm…_ (e.g., _I'm Pablo_.) But on the phone, _it's_ is used (e.g., _Hi, Leo. It's Max_.) Be careful that students don't confuse the two.

- Next, get students to think about what they say when they get a phone call, but they don't know who the caller is. What do they say in their own language? Then direct students' attention again to the Useful Language box. Model saying _Excuse me, who's calling?_ Note for students that _Who_ is used to ask about people, and _Who's_ is a contraction of _Who is_.

- Finally, direct students' attention to the Word Bank. Have students use their dictionaries to learn the words _different, new_, and _sorry_. Note that "Sorry!" is a shortened form of the apology "I'm sorry." Point out that _yeah_ is an informal way of saying _yes_. Say each word aloud and have students repeat.

**B** 🔊 Track 23 Read and listen to the conversation.

- Have students read the dialogue and then play the audio once through. For additional practice, play the conversation again and have students repeat each line.

**C** 🔄 Work with a partner. Say the conversation in **B**.

- Have students work in pairs to practice the conversation. After they've done it once, have them change roles and practice again.

**D** Cover the Useful Language box in **A** and the conversation in **B**. Read the conversations below. Guess the words.

- Tell students to cover the Useful Language box and the conversation in **B**, modeling this for them so they know what to do. Then tell students to look at the two short conversations in **D**. Can they guess any of the words? Tell them to write their answers.

**E** 🔊 Track 24 Listen. Write the words and the phone numbers.

- Play the audio. Students should check their answers in **D**, and write the correct words and phone numbers. Note: In conversation 2, the speaker says "your number isn't in my phone." Point out to students that it's common to shorten *phone number* to just *number*.

**Answers**
Conversation 1  A: Hello, who's   B: It's, 702-1639
Conversation 2  A: Hello, who's, 916-8077   B: your

**F** 🔄 Work with a partner. Say the conversations in **D**.

- Have students work with their partner to practice saying each conversation in **D**.

**G** Think of a new name and phone number.

- Each student should make up a new name and phone number.

**H** 🔄 Sit back-to-back with a partner. Say the conversation in **B** again.

**STUDENT A:** Answer the phone. Write the caller's name and phone number.
**STUDENT B:** Use your name and phone number from **G**.

- Point out the image and have students read the speech bubbles. Elicit the rest of the conversation. Then model the activity with a student volunteer. Write the following on the board:

Caller: _____
Phone number: _____

- Review the conversation in **B** with the class. Then stand back to back with the student and role play the conversation in **B** again. If you've got your phone, take it out and pretend to call the student. He or she should answer. When the student asks who's calling, give your name and elicit the next line of the conversation from the student (the class can help him or her as necessary). Complete the conversation and give the student your number. The student should write your name on the board next to "Caller" and your phone number. Have the class check that the student wrote the information correctly.

- Then put students in pairs and have them sit back to back. Have them role play the conversation in **B** again. Student A should write the caller's name and phone number. When they're done, Student B should check that Student A wrote the information correctly.

**I** 🔄 Change roles. Repeat **H**.

- Have students change roles and have the conversation again. Encourage them to try and say it without looking at their books.

**J** 🔄 Repeat **H** and **I** with a different partner.

- Assign students to new pairs to repeat **H** and **I**. This time, ask them to do it with books closed.

**LANGUAGE NOTE**  In this Speaking activity, students learn how to answer the phone. You can also introduce simple language for ending a phone call in English.

*A: Talk to you later. / See you (later).*
*B: OK. Bye.*

# 5 MY NEIGHBORHOOD

## 1 VOCABULARY

In this Vocabulary lesson, students will learn to identify and talk about places in a neighborhood.

**A** 🔊 **Track 25** Listen and repeat.

- Say the title of the unit (*My Neighborhood*) aloud with students. Then have them look up the word *neighborhood* in their dictionaries so they understand the meaning. Ask students to name a neighborhood in your city. (Make sure that students understand the meaning of the word *city.*) Then have them look at the large background photo and read the caption. Ask students: Is your neighborhood the same or different?

- Next, have students look at the list of words in the box (*ATM, bank, bus stop,* etc.). Tell students to find each place in the photos on the page. Give them a minute or so to do this. Then play the audio. As the speaker says a word, students should repeat it and point to the picture on the page.

- At the end, point to photo 11 (*store*) and direct students to the Word Bank. Write on the board: *This is a… store.* Ask students to call out the type of store (*clothing, book, department store*). Ask students to name a bookstore and department store in your city or another.

### PRONUNCIATION TIP

Note the different sounds of the letter *o* in these words:
stop, shop: /ɑ/
coffee, office, store /ɔ/
movie, school: /u/
post: /oʊ/

**LANGUAGE NOTE** ATM is an abbreviation for *automated teller machine.* It's said letter by letter (A-T-M).

- Many of the vocabulary items are compound words, that is, they are made up of two words written separately (*bus stop, coffee shop, post office, movie theater*) or joined together (*supermarket*). They're always spoken as a single unit.

- It can also be helpful to point out to students that in many of these compound nouns, the stress falls on the first word, so we say <u>post</u> office, <u>coffee</u> shop, and <u>supermarket.</u> Have students practice saying these words with the appropriate stress. Also, point out that *bus stop* almost sounds like a single word (due to the linking of the *s* sounds). Have students practice saying it.

**ADDITIONAL VOCABULARY** Other types of common stores in the United States:

*Drugstore/pharmacy*: In the United States, this store sells medicine and other basic household items.

*Convenience store*: This is a store (like 7–11) that sells snacks, drinks, and other simple foods along with basic household items. It's usually smaller than a supermarket and is open late.

**B** Write the words.

- Have students look at item 1 and make sure they know what to do. Then have them work on their own to unscramble the letters and write each word. Have them check answers with a partner, saying and spelling each word aloud and pointing to the picture (1–12) it corresponds to.

**CHALLENGE** 1. Make this a timed activity by giving students two minutes to complete it. 2. Have individual students play against a partner to see who can finish first. 3. Have students cover the word list and do the exercise.

1. park  2. gym  3. school  4. bank  5. post office
6. bus stop  7. store  8. restaurant  9. ATM  10. cafe
11. theater  12. supermarket

**C** 🔁 Work with a partner.

1. Cover the word list.

2. Ask and answer the question.

• Give students a minute or so to study the pictures 1–12 again. Then tell them to cover the word list. Model the example with a student. Students should take turns pointing to different pictures and asking and answering the question *What's this?* with a partner.

**CHALLENGE** Have students quiz each other in a "rapid fire round" by asking and answering as fast as they can.

**D** 🔊 Track 26 Listen to the phone calls. Circle the answer.

• Before students listen, have them preview the sentences. Introduce the word *home* in item 1a. Also draw students' attention to the use of *at + location* and point out its usage. After students listen, have them check answers in pairs.

**LANGUAGE NOTE** Use *at the* + location to talk about where a person is: *at the store, at the gym, at the park*. There are a few exceptions to this rule however, usually for familiar places that we often visit or stay in. In these cases, you only use the preposition *at* (without *the*): *at school, at work, at home*. Students should memorize these exceptions.

**Answers**
1. a  2. c  3. b

**E** 🔁 Say your ideas. Use two places from the word list.

• Say the word *favorite* in the Word Bank with students and make sure they understand its meaning. Then have students choose two places from the word list and complete the sentence (*My favorite __ is __*).

**PRONUNCIATION TIP**

Write *favorite* on the board and cross out the *o*. Say *favorite* and explain to students that most people pronounce only 2 syllables.

**SUPPORT** To get students started, you can also put these ideas on the board:

My favorite…

1. cafe / coffee shop is…

2. store is…

3. park is…

4. restaurant is…

Share your favorite places and elicit some from students.

# 2 GRAMMAR

This Grammar lesson will focus on the use of *there is / there are* followed by singular and plural nouns.

**A** Look at the pictures. Say the words.

• Review the language at the bottom of the four photos. The important thing here is for students to understand the meaning of the different words (*a, some, no,* and numbers) and when to use the singular vs. the plural forms of the nouns that follow.

**LANGUAGE NOTE** 1. It's also possible to say *There is no tree (here)* this lesson focuses on *There are no* with plural nouns. 2. Make sure students understand that *There is a tree* has the same meaning as *There is one tree.* Since the latter is typically used to emphasize singularity and therefore less commonly used, encourage students to use *a/ an* when referring to a single item throughout the lesson (unless otherwise indicated).

**B** Study the chart.

• This lesson only focuses on the following structures:

    *There is a/an* + singular count noun
    *There are two/three/four…* + plural count noun
    *There are no* + plural count noun
    *There are some* + plural count noun

• The following patterns are also common in English, but will not be introduced here: *There's no* + singular count noun, *There aren't any* + plural count noun, and *There are a lot of/many* + plural count noun.

- Point out the Notice! note and that there is no written contracted form for the plural (*there are*).

- Introduce <u>on my street</u> and <u>in my neighborhood</u> as phrases for students to memorize.

**LANGUAGE NOTE** If appropriate, explain that *on* is used to indicate the surface of something. Give students the example: *It's on the desk.* The usage here of *in* indicates a location/place. Give students the example: *We're in our classroom.*

- Read through the sentences in the grammar chart. Ask students to listen and repeat. Then have individual students practice reading the sentences.

**PRONUNCIATION TIP**

*a* and *an* are pronounced /eɪ/ and /æn/ when they are alone. However, they are pronounced /ə/ and /ən/ in a sentence.

- Then, do a quick review of the vocabulary students have learned in the previous lesson (*bank, school,* etc.)

**PREP WORK** Write these words in one column on the board: *a/an, some, no,* and *one/two/three...* In a second column, write some, or all, of the new vocabulary words students have suggested. In a third column, simply write *street* and *neighborhood.*

- Point to one item in each column (e.g., *a/an, school, neighborhood*) and say the sentences (*There's a school in my neighborhood*) as students repeat. Do this with two or three examples. Next, point to different words from each column but don't say the sentence. Students should come up with the answer as a group. With later sentences, you can ask individual students to come up with the correct answers.

**CHALLENGE** A third and more difficult step would be for you to point to items in the first and third columns only (e.g., *no, street*) and students have to choose a place from the second column and construct their own sentence (e.g., *There are no gyms on my street.*)

**C** Circle the answers.

- Have students read through the sentences silently. Make sure they understand all the vocabulary.

**ADDITIONAL VOCABULARY** *good, near*

- Give students some time to do the exercise. Then go over the answers together. For item 5, ask if students can say the sentence in another way. (Answer: *There's a department store on Main Street.*)

**Answers**
1. There's   2. There are   3. there are   4. There are
5. There's

**D** 🔀 Correct the sentences.

- Put students into pairs. Tell them that there is an error in each sentence. Ask them to rewrite the sentences to make them correct.

**PREP WORK** While students are doing the exercise, write the incorrect examples (as they are printed in the Student Book) on the board. When students are finished with the activity, have different pairs come to the board and write their corrections for the class. Check to make sure everyone has the correct grammar and spelling before moving on to the next item.

**Answers**
1. There are no parks   2. There's a restaurant
3. There are no gyms   4. There are some banks
5. There are three cafes   6. There are two supermarkets.

**E** 🔊 Track 27 Look at the picture. Listen and read.

- Ask students to look at the picture. Before you listen or read, point to different things in the picture as students tell you what they are. It's OK if they don't know the answer at this point. The words in the drawing that students know are *park, tree, school, movie theater,* and *street.*

**ADDITIONAL VOCABULARY** *car, garage, building*

- Next play the audio as students read along. For a second listening, you can ask students to tap their desks as they follow the rhythm of each sentence.

**F** 🔊 Track 27 Listen again. Point to the places in **E**.

- Play the audio again. Students should point to the places mentioned in **E** as they listen. You may also pause after each sentence to allow students time to repeat (silently and then out loud).

**PREP WORK** Project the map onto the board or a wall. Read the sentences in random order and have individual students come to the board and point out the correct item on the map.

**CHALLENGE** Review *yes / no* questions by asking students about the information presented in **E**. All of your questions should be in the singular and students should answer accordingly. For example,

> *Is there a park on High Street?*
> (Answer: *Yes, there's a park.*)
> *Is there a tree in the park?*
> (Answer: *Yes, there <u>are</u> **some** trees in the park.*)
> The last one is the trickiest: *Is there a garage?*
> (Answer: *No, there are no garages.*)

**G** 🔋 Cover the sentences in **E**. Take turns with a partner.

**STUDENT A**: Say a sentence about the picture.

**STUDENT B**: Say a different sentence about the picture.

- Students should cover the sentences below the map in **E** and practice identifying different items using *There is* or *There are.*

**H** 🔋 Draw a picture of your street. Use these words. Tell your partner.

- Give students time to draw a simple map of their street, a street they know or a neighborhood. (If they don't have room in their textbooks, have them draw the map on a separate piece of paper.) Tell them they must use four or five of the vocabulary words they've learned on their map. They should be prepared to talk about their map and use all of the different sentence structures using *There is* and *There are.*

- Put students in pairs and have them explain their maps to a partner.

**CHALLENGE** 1. Increase the number of vocabulary items students are required to put on their maps. 2. Tell students not to label the places on their map. Students then take turns asking questions about their partner's map using the question form *Is there a/an...?* (The student will either answer *Yes* and point to the place on the map or *No*).

**EXPANSION** Tell students to not put their names on their maps. Once they have finished doing some pair work, ask each student to tape his/her map to the wall. Students should circulate around the room looking at all the maps. Have students vote on their favorite map (the voting can be done through a process of elimination or by a single vote) and then reveal the winner!

# 3 SPEAKING

In this Speaking lesson, students will practice asking for and giving directions in English.

**A** Say the sentences in the Useful Language box with the teacher.

- Have students look at the photo and guide them to see that the woman is asking the man for directions. Pretend that you need to ask someone on the street for directions. Call out *Excuse me?* to model how we get someone's attention. Point out this expression in the Useful Language box, and have students repeat it after you.

- Next, point out how one asks for directions: *Is there a... around here?* Explain that *around here* means *in this area.*

- Then introduce *go straight, turn left, turn right* using the graphic on the page, and have students repeat these directions after you.

- Draw students' attention to the use of...
  **on** + street: *Turn left <u>on Jay street</u>.*
  **on the left / right**: *The ATM is <u>on the left</u>* (side of the street).

**LANGUAGE NOTE** We typically use *Is there a...?* to ask about a generic location: *Is there an ATM / a post office around here?*

We don't typically use *Is there a...?* to ask about a specific place with a proper name:

~~Is there Ming's Café around here?~~   ~~Is there Olympic Park around here?~~

We say: *Is Ming's Café around here?*
*Is Olympic Park around here?*

**B** 🔊 Track 28 Read and listen to the conversation.

- Have students read the dialogue and then play the audio once through. For additional practice, play the dialogue again and have students repeat each line.

**C** Where is the ATM? Circle the number.

- Introduce the word *where* and make sure students understand its meaning. (We use *where* to ask about the location of something.) Then have students read the dialogue in **B** again and follow the directions. They should circle the place on the map where the ATM is. Check the answer as a class.

**CHALLENGE** Have students cover the conversation in **B** and listen and follow the directions given.

**Answer**
The ATM is number 4 on the map.

**D** 🔁 Say the conversation in **B**.

- Have students work in pairs to practice the conversation in **B**. After they've done it once, have them change roles and practice again. While students are doing this, put the following dialogue on the board:

  A: Excuse me?
  B: Yes?
  A: Is there an ATM around here?
  B: An ATM? Um, sorry, I don't know.
  A: OK, thanks. *(asks another person)* Excuse me? Is there an ATM around here?
  C: Yeah. Go straight and turn right on Jay Street. The ATM is on the left.
  A: Great, thanks!

- Ask two student volunteers to come to the front of the class. You should be speaker B and the students should be speakers A and C. Role play the dialogue for the class. When you get to the line where you say: *An ATM? Um, sorry, I don't know* model the meaning of *I don't know* for the class (e.g., by shrugging your shoulders). Point out that this is what we say when we don't know an answer to a question. (This language is also given in the Useful Language box.) Then continue on with the dialogue. After you've finished, rotate roles and perform the dialogue a few more times with different students.

- Have students work in a group of three to practice the dialogue on the board. Then have them change roles and practice again.

**EXPANSION** DISAPPEARING DIALOGUE After students are done practicing, erase some of the words in the dialogue on the board, for example:

  A: _____ me?
  B: Yes?
  A: Is _____ an ATM _____ here?
  B: An ATM? Um, sorry, I don't _____.

A: OK, thanks. *(asks another person)* Excuse me? Is _____ an ATM _____ here?
C: Yeah. _____ straight and _____ right on Jay Street. The ATM is _____ the left.
A: Great, thanks!

- Tell students to look at the dialogue on the board and say it again. Can they remember the words? After they finish, erase some more words, and tell students to say it again. Keep doing this until you've erased almost all of the words, except *ATM* and *Jay Street*. See how much students are able to remember. Encourage them to use the expressions in the Useful Language box and the map to help them.

**E** 🔊 Track 29 Where are the six places? Listen. Write the number of each place (1–6) on the map.

- Before students listen, have them look at the names of the six places. Make sure they understand the meaning of *subway station* and *gas station.* Say these two new places and have students repeat. For this exercise, students should listen, follow the directions, and number the places (1–6) on the map correctly. Play the audio and have students listen to the first set of directions as they trace the route on the map to the subway station (marked "1" on the map; the answer is given). Stop the audio and make sure everyone understands the activity. Then resume playing the audio for items 2–6.

**NOTICE** For this activity to work, each time a speaker gives directions, the starting point is the"You are here" point on the map. Make sure students understand this.

**Answers**

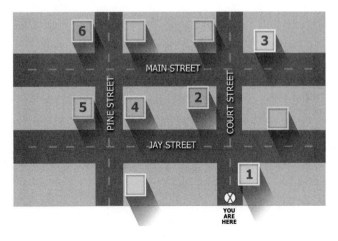

**F** 🔁 Work with a partner. Take turns. Ask for directions to three places on the map.

- Point out the speech bubbles and model the activity with a student. Have students take turns asking about three places on the map. The student's partner should give the directions. It might help to assign students the places they should ask for:
  Student A: Ask about the *subway station*, *supermarket*, and *bookstore*.
  Student B: Ask about the *coffee shop*, *gas station*, and *post office*.

**G** 🔁 Draw two more places on your map.

**STUDENT A:** a bus stop, a drugstore
**STUDENT B:** a park, a library

- Say the words *drugstore* and *library* in the Word Bank with students and make sure they understand their meaning. Then have students add two more places to their own map. Student A should draw a bus stop and a drugstore on his or her map. Student B should draw a park and a library.

**H** 🔁 Ask for directions to the places on your partner's map. Draw them on your map.

- Student A should now ask Student B for directions to the park and library. Student B should give directions to these places and Student A should note them on his or her map. Then Student B should ask Student A for directions to the bus stop and drug store. Student A should give directions to these places and Student B should note them on his or her map.

**EXPANSION** Have students take turns asking each other about the places near their school: subway station, bus stop, ATM, coffee shop, post office. They can also add their own ideas.

- Students should take turns asking for and giving each other directions. If they don't know where something is located in the neighborhood, they can say *Sorry, I don't know*. If the place doesn't exist in the area around their school, point out to students that they can say *No, there's no... around here*. (e.g., *No, there's no post office around here*.)

# 6 COUNTRIES

## 1 VOCABULARY

In this Vocabulary lesson, students will learn to say countries and nationalities in English.

**A** 🔊 **Track 30** Listen and say the countries and nationalities.

- Preteach the word *country.* Before students open their books, ask them *What country are you in now? What do you call people from your country?* See if students know how to say their country and nationality in English.

- Next, ask them to name as many countries as they can in one minute in their own language. Write these on the board. Then ask students if they know the names of those countries in English. It's not important that they know all of them as this is just a lead-in exercise.

- Have students open their books and cover the chart so that only the flags are exposed. Do they know any of these flags? Which countries are they?

- Have students uncover the chart. First, read through the list of *country names* while students listen. Say, *I am from (country name).* Then do the same with the list of nationalities. At the end of the list, say *I'm (nationality).* Make sure students understand the distinction. Finally, play the audio and have students listen and repeat.

- Draw the students' attention to the change in stress patterns between the country and nationality words. For example, we say CHIna but then ChiNESE. One way to highlight this is to play the audio again and have students underline the stressed syllable in each word. Go over answers in class.

---

### PRONUNCIATION TIP

Note that many of the countries and nationalities have unstressed vowels that are reduced to /ə/:

China
Japan - Japanese
Portugal - Portuguese
Australia - Australian
Vietnamese
Brazil - Brazilian
Peru - Peruvian
Canada - Canadian
Korea - Korean
Mexican
The United States - American
Venezuela - Venezuelan
The United Kingdom
Sweden

---

**LANGUAGE NOTE** Point out that the United States is often referred to simply as "the U.S." and the United Kingdom as "the UK." The United Kingdom is made up of England, Scotland, Wales, and Northern Ireland.

**CHALLENGE** Introduce some other countries that don't fit into one of the patterns presented in the chart.
*the Dominican Republic / Dominican*
*France / French*
*Greece / Greek*
*Thailand / Thai*
*the Netherlands / Dutch*

**B** 🔄 Work with a partner.
- Cover the nationalities in the chart.
- Take turns: Say a country. Then say the nationality.

- For this exercise, students will cover the list of nationalities in the chart and take turns quizzing each other. Circulate and assist as necessary.

**EXPANSION** Play an "Around the World" game to test the students' vocabulary knowledge. While one student remains seated, ask another student to stand by the seated student's desk. Tell them that you will say a country name and the first student to call out the correct nationality wins and advances by moving to stand next to the next seated student in the row. (The student who loses either remains seated or takes the seat if he or she was standing.) In this way a student who wins a lot of "battles" will advance around the room or travel "around the world." After you've played the game for a few minutes, stop and ask your students to count how many desks they have moved around the classroom. The student who has traveled the most number of seats wins the game.

**CHALLENGE** After playing a few rounds in this way, start calling out both country names or nationalities and students have to give their opposites.

**C** Complete the sentences. Use words from the chart.

- Before starting the exercise, draw students' attention to the words in the Word Bank. Use the photos on the page to define the words *flag* and *soup*. For the other words, say *In France, there's the French language.* If you have a map in the room, you can point to France as you are speaking.

- Also, make sure that students understand the meaning of these words in item four: *over* (meaning *more than*) and *people* (one person, two people).

- Preteach the names of the "continents" *Europe* and *Asia* that appear in item seven.

**ADDITIONAL VOCABULARY** Teach students other words for large land masses (*Africa, North America, South America, Australia*). Then ask them to name a country (in English) that goes under each heading. (Obviously, for *Australia* there is only one answer!)

- Have students look at the Notice! information. Remind them that in the same way we talk about location by saying *in my neighborhood*, we also use the preposition *in* with city and country names. Demonstrate this by saying where you are, for example: *I'm in Lima. Lima is in Peru.*

- Tell students they are going to take a quiz. Before they begin, read through the sentences together.

Then have them fill in their answers. At the end, ask students to put their pens down and tell them they are going to listen to check their answers.

**SUPPORT** To make the quiz easier, you can write this information about the quiz answers on the board ahead of time:

Questions 1, 2, 3, 4, 6, 7, and 10 → city and country names

Questions 5, 8, and 9 → nationalities

**CHALLENGE** Time the quiz. Give students one to two minutes to complete it.

*Variation:* Review the content of the quiz together as a class and then have students close their books. Divide the class into teams of five or ten students each (since there are ten questions on the quiz). For the first question, have each team send a representative to the board. Read the question aloud and give the students at the board time to write their answers. Note: During this step, the other team members cannot help in any way and the students at the board should be careful not to spy on other students, while they should cover their answers with their hands. On the count of three, ask the students to reveal their answers. Give each team a point if their representative got the answer right. Continue with different students coming to the board until you have gone through all the questions in the quiz. At the end of this game, you can still play the audio (in Exercise **D**) to make sure everyone has understood the correct answers.

**EXPANSION** After completing the quiz, return to item 3, which mentions languages. Ask your students what other languages, if any, are spoken in their own country.

**D** 🔊 Track 31 Listen and check your answers in **C**.

- Play the audio for students to check their answers to the quiz. If you haven't played the game and already awarded points, here is where you can do so. Give students one point for each correct answer. Some of the words are difficult to spell, so you may want to give them the point if they were "close" in their spelling. Just make certain that everyone has the words spelled correctly once you've finished.

**Answers**
1. Tokyo   2. Australia   3. Canada   4. China
5. Vietnamese   6. the UK   7. Turkey   8. Portuguese
9. Peruvian   10. Mexico

**E** 🔄 Work with a partner. Write three sentences. Use the sentences in **C** as a model.

- In pairs students are going to make their own mini-quizzes by writing three sentences (similar to the ones they've seen in **C** above). Note: Students can use the countries and nationalities in this lesson as well as ones not featured here. Circulate and provide students with the necessary language as needed so that they can write their sentences.

**SUPPORT** You may want to choose three of the simpler sentences and put them on the board. For students who are struggling, they can go with these ideas:

_____ is a city in _____.
_____ is the main language in _____.
_____ is _____.
(famous person)          (nationality)

**F** 👥 Work with another pair. Say your sentences in **E**. (Do not say the country or nationality.) The other pair guesses.

- Once all the sentences have been written, ask each pair of students to join another pair. Taking turns, they should read their sentences while their partners try to guess the correct answers. Once both pairs have finished, have half of the pairs rotate to form new groups and play the game again.

- As a follow-up, if any new vocabulary (especially around the language of countries and nationalities) has emerged from this exercise, write it on the board so that the entire class can learn it.

# 2 GRAMMAR

This Grammar lesson will introduce adjectives and focus on two similar patterns: 1) *be* + adjective (*It's beautiful*) and *be* + adjective + noun (*It's a beautiful city*).

**A** Look at the pictures. Say the words.

- At the start, students are introduced to six words that are used to describe cities: *big, small, old, exciting, beautiful,* and *interesting* (in the Word Bank). Spend some time on the pronunciation of these words, especially *beautiful* (/ˈbju·tɪ·fəl/), *exciting*

(/s/ sound for the letter *c*), and *interesting* (often said with only three syllables, not four, /ˈɪn·trə·stɪŋ/).

**ADDITIONAL VOCABULARY** If appropriate for your group, introduce other adjectives used to describe places, such as *crowded* and *popular*.

**B** Study the chart.

- Read the sentences in the chart aloud. Ask students to tap out the stress and rhythm of the sentences as you read. Read the sentences and ask your students to repeat.

- Get students to notice the word order in the chart, that is, that adjectives (words like *big, small, interesting*) come after *is* and *are*.

- Substitute a different city (e.g., *Sao Paulo* or *Tokyo*) for *New York* in the chart. Invite individual students to say a new sentence and write it on the board (e.g., *Sao Paulo is beautiful* or *Sao Paulo is small*). Ask the class to raise their hands if they agree with this statement. After several students have made sentences, move on to the plural noun *neighborhoods* and have students make more sentences.

**C** Write the missing letters.

- Explain that these words have missing letters. Give students time to write them in. (This works best if you have students cover up the words in **A** and **B**.)

**CHALLENGE** Timed activity. Have students start the exercise with their books closed. On the count of three, have them open their books and begin. Students will be racing against each other.

**SUPPORT** If spelling is particularly challenging for students, write the vowels *a, e, i, o,* and *u* on the board. Tell students that they should choose from this set when filling in the missing letters.

- A more dynamic way to review the spelling is to have individual students come to the board and write out the words. With the class, check for errors.

**EXPANSION** After you've finished the exercise, hold a spelling bee. You can put students into groups of four with one group as the leader (reading the words) while the other students take turns spelling a word. If a student makes a mistake or doesn't finish within a certain time, they are out. Play several rounds. If you want to give your students more practice in spelling the words, play a game where you call out a word and two students have to race to the board and write it down correctly.

1. int<u>e</u>res<u>ti</u>ng   2. <u>o</u>ld   3. b<u>ig</u>   4. <u>e</u>xc<u>i</u>ting   5. sm<u>all</u>
6. b<u>eau</u>tif<u>u</u>l

**D**  Complete the sentences. Then match 1, 2, and 3 with a picture.

- Introduce two new adjectives from the Word Bank: *famous* and *fun*. Then have students look at the three photos of the cities *London, Rio de Janeiro,* and *Moscow*. Elicit the names of the countries the cities are in and their nationalities (Russia/Russian is the only one students haven't seen in this unit). Write a sentence like this on the board: *It's exciting.* Then take a class poll. As you point to each picture, students should raise their hand for the city that looks exciting. (Each student can only vote once.) The adjectives *beautiful* and *interesting* also work well with this activity.

- When you move on to doing the actual exercise, explain to students that they will sometimes be completing words (e.g., *It's int<u>eresting</u>*) as well as writing complete words: *It's in Brazil*). Students should understand that each set of sentences describes one of the cities pictured.

- Give students time to complete the sentences and then put them in pairs to check their answers. The same pair of students should then match each set of sentences to one of the cities. After everyone has finished, go over the answers with the class. Make sure to check spelling and correct use of apostrophes.

**EXPANSION**  To make the matching portion of the exercise more fun, assign a city name to each corner of the classroom. Then read each of the sentences in random order. Students listen and then have to go and stand in the appropriate city (i.e., corner of the room) that the sentence describes. For example, if you say *The parties are fun*, students would stand in the Rio corner. If you say *It's in England*, they would move to the London corner. Continue until all of the sentences have been read aloud.

Answers
1. It's int<u>e</u>resting. It<u>'s</u> in Russia. The subway stations <u>are</u> beautiful. **Answer:** Moscow
2. It<u>'s</u> exciting. The parties <u>are</u> fun. It's <u>in</u> Brazil. **Answer:** Rio de Janeiro
3. It<u>'s</u> in England. There<u>'s</u> a clock. It's fam<u>ous</u>. It's <u>o</u>ld. **Answer:** London

**E**  Study the chart.

- This second chart shows students that adjectives can come before nouns as well. The same rules

apply as in the first chart (the adjectives follow *am, is,* and *are*). Point out that with the singular nouns, students must remember to include *a/an* in their sentence: *New York is an interesting city.*

- First read the sentences in the chart aloud as students tap out the rhythm and stress. Then read and have the students repeat.

**F**  🔊 Track 32  PRONUNCIATION Listen and repeat.

**LANGUAGE NOTE**  Content words (nouns, main verbs, adjectives, etc.) are usually emphasized, whereas structure words (pronouns, the verb *be, a/an,* etc.) are not. You can show this to students by first having them listen to you read the four sentences aloud. Ask them if they notice any difference in the stress of certain words.

- Next read the sentences as you tap out the stress pattern on your desk. Students should notice that the structure words (in regular type on the page) are represented by lighter and quicker taps, while the content words (in boldfaced type) are slower and heavier.

- Play the audio. Have students listen and repeat. Explain the Word Bank words as necessary by giving examples.

**G**  Rewrite the sentences. Add the new words.

- Go over the eight sentences together. First, read them aloud. Then practice reading them together. Make sure students understand the meaning of the sentences.

**ADDITIONAL VOCABULARY**  *building* (if it wasn't introduced in Unit 5) and *island*

- Go over the first example together and then give students time to rewrite the sentences. (These sentences are also recycling some past grammar points, such as *there is/there are* and possessive adjectives, which demonstrates to students that adjectives can show up in all kinds of sentences.) Note that both items 2 and 8 require students to switch the article from *a* to *an* (or vice versa).

**CLASSROOM MANAGEMENT**  There are a lot of sentences to cover. If necessary, split them up and give each student only 1 or 2 sentences to write. As students finish writing, have a volunteer put his or her sentence on the board. Then go over the answers as a group.

**EXPANSION**  Once the sentences are on the board, review the pronunciation point by asking students to circle the words in each sentence that they think carry more stress. In the Answer Key that follows, the stressed words are in bold.

**Answers**
1. There are some **interesting neighborhoods** in **Los Angeles**. 2. She's an **English teacher**. 3. It's my **new phone**. 4. **Lima** is a **big city**. 5. They're her **beautiful pictures**. 6. There are no **old buildings**. 7. There's a **famous restaurant** on my **street**. 8. **Ibiza** is a **Spanish island**.

**H** Work with a partner. Think of a place. Write 3–4 sentences about the place. Use words like *big, fun, interesting*.

- Review the example sentences about Disney World. Explain to students that they are going to be choosing their own place and writing about it. They should use the example sentences as a model.

- Students should work in pairs to complete this activity. It works best if they think of a well-known place that others can guess. The place can be a country, city, (theme) park, shopping mall, café/restaurant, or anywhere else. Give each pair time to write down three or four sentences and encourage them to use adjectives. Circulate and answer any questions students may have.

**I** Join another pair. Say your sentences. Your partners guess.

- Put pairs together. If numbers are uneven, you can always put three pairs together. Each pair should read their sentences about their place while the other pair guesses. (For this to work, students should be careful not to let the other pair see their sentences beforehand.) After both pairs have finished, you can have one pair of students rotate to form a new group and play the game again.

# 3 SPEAKING

In this Speaking lesson, students will practice asking where people are from and explaining why a place is famous.

**A** Say the sentences in the Useful Language box with the teacher.

- Have students look at the photo and read the caption. Ask: *Where is this place, in what country?*

Then get them to think about which adjective(s) from the Grammar page they'd use to describe the park in the photo (e.g., *beautiful, old*).

**CULTURE NOTE** Suzhou (pronounced *Soo-jō*), China is a city about 85 kilometers (about 53 miles) west of Shanghai. It's famous for its historic architecture, canals, bridges, and especially its "classical gardens," many of which have been declared World Heritage sites.

- Next, have students look at the Useful Language box and model asking and answering the questions with different students. Remind students that they learned the word *where* in Unit 5. (It's used to ask about the location of something.) Note that when someone asks *Where are you from?* you can answer with a country name only (e.g., *China.*) To get more specific information, a person might ask *Where in…* (e.g., *Where in China? I'm from Suzhou.*)

**LANGUAGE NOTE** USING NEAR When we talk about a town or city that people might not know well, it's common to mention a better-known city for reference using *near*, for example, *I'm from Suzhou. It's near (close to) Shanghai*. Introduce the word *near* to students and make sure they understand the meaning.

- Finally, direct students to the sentences used for describing a city and what it's famous for, and say them aloud with the class. Remind students that they learned the word *famous* in the grammar lesson. Elicit examples about other cities.

**PRONUNCIATION TIP**

Help students notice that in *famous* /ˈfeɪ·məs/, the *a* is /eɪ/ and the *ou* letters are reduced to /ə/.

**LANGUAGE NOTE** FAMOUS FOR When we explain why a place is famous, it's common to use these structures. Direct students' attention to them in the Useful Language box.

- *famous for* + *its* + noun: *Paris is **famous for** its food / museums*.

- *famous for* + proper noun: *Paris is **famous for** the Eiffel Tower*.

**B** 🔊 **Track 33** Read and listen to the conversation.

- Have students read the dialogue and then play the audio once through. For additional practice, play the dialogue again and have students repeat each line.

**C** 🔄 Work with a partner. Answer the questions.

- Have students answer the three questions with a partner. Practice saying these country and city names with students aloud: *the Dominican Republic, Shanghai.*

**EXPANSION** Have students look at the photo at the top of the page. Point out that it's one of the many beautiful parks in Suzhou. Have them find other photos of gardens and parks in this city online. Tell them to also find photos of the Dominican Republic online. Which place is interesting to them?

**Answers**
1. the Dominican Republic   2. Suzhou, China
3. Suzhou is famous for its beautiful parks.

**D** 🔄 Work with a partner. Say the conversation in **B**.

- Have students work in pairs to practice the conversation in **B**. After they've done it once, have them change roles and practice again.

**E** Complete the sentences.

- Have students work on their own to complete the two sentences. In sentence two:

1. tell students they can talk about more than one thing their city is famous for.

2. encourage students to use adjectives in their sentences (e.g., *My city is famous for its beautiful beaches / exciting nightlife.*)

**CLASSROOM MANAGEMENT** If most (or all) of your students are from the same city or area, tell them to choose a different city in their country or the world, or assign students different cities, and have them complete the sentences in **E**. Give students time to research their city.

**ADDITIONAL VOCABULARY** A city can be famous for its *food, parks, architecture, music, beaches, museums, schools, nightlife, sports team,* and many other things. Introduce vocabulary as needed to help students talk about their city, and put all ideas on the board.

**EXPANSION** Have students find photos or video of their city showing what it's famous for.

**F** 🔄 Say the conversation in **B** again. Use your ideas in **E**.

- Model the conversation with a student and give information about your city. Assign students to new pairs, and have them practice the dialogue in **B** again using their sentences in **E**.

**EXPANSION** Have students create a short presentation or poster about their city (or a city you assign them). They should explain what it's famous for using text, photos, and video. Then have students give their presentation to a small group. Put this language on the board to get them started: *This is <name of city>. It's famous for…* At the end, have students rank the cities they learned about from 1 (my favorite city) to 4.

**G** Read the name in the chart. Where is the man from? Write his country and nationality.

- Have students read the information in the chart. Can they guess which country this pop singer is from by looking at the city he's from? If not, give students the answer. (*Justin Bieber is from Canada.*) Then ask what his nationality is. Tell students to write both in the chart.

**H** Complete the chart in **G**. Use your phone to help you.

1. Write the names of four famous people from different countries.

2. Write the person's country and nationality.

3. Write the city the person is from.

- Tell students to research four famous people from different countries to complete the chart. They can use their phones to help them.

**SUPPORT** Prepare some personal profiles of famous people before class and give each student one or two of the profiles to work with. Instead of having four people to research, students will only have to research two or three.

**I** 🎲 Work in a group. Play the game. Take turns.

1. Choose a person in your chart.

2. Ask your partners: *Where is… from?*

3. The first person with the correct answer gets 1 point.

4. Then ask him or her: *Where in…?*

5. A correct answers gets 1 point.

- Put students in groups of three or four. One person in each group should be the scorekeeper. Point out the examples in the speech bubbles. Then model how to play the game with one of the groups.

1. Choose a name from your chart. Ask your partners the question: *Where is... from?*

2. Your groupmates compete to be the first to call out the person's country or nationality (e.g., *He's from Canada. He's Canadian.*) The person who guesses correctly gets one point.

3. If someone guesses the correct country, then ask about the famous person's city (e.g., *Yes, he's from Canada. Where in Canada?*) An additional correct guess gets one point.

4. Do this with all names in your chart. Then it's another player's turn.

5. At the end, the person with the most points wins.

- Another option for playing the game is to have students write each answer on a piece of paper and then turn their papers over at the same time. Students receive a point for each correct answer.

# PUT IT TOGETHER 2

## 1 GRAMMAR

This Grammar lesson will introduce *Wh-* questions with *be* and contrast them with *Yes / No* questions with *be* (which students have already learned).

**A** Study the chart.

**LANGUAGE NOTE** This unit will introduce *wh-* question words that are used to ask about:

information or things (*what*)
place or position (*where*)
a person's identity (*who*)

This unit does not touch on *wh-* question words used to ask about: date and time (*when*), reasons (*why*), the way to do something (*how*), possession (*whose*), and information about specific things (*which*). These will be focused on in later units.

- Students learned *Yes / No* questions with *be* in *Put It Together 1.* To do a quick review of those questions and the short answers that follow (with books closed), ask different students questions like these:
  *Is she* (or *he*) *your classmate? Is she your teacher? Is she your friend?*
  *Are you in New York? Are you in* (current location)? *Are you in class? Are you at home?*
  *Is it a clock? Is it a cell phone? Are these keys?*

- After they have answered a few *Yes / No* questions correctly, write this question on the board: *Is it a computer?* Introduce the question word *what* and explain how it is used. Then write the word *What* in front of the sentence on the board, change *Is* to *is* and cross out the words *a computer.* (You should now see the question *What is it* on the board.) In this way, students can see that *Wh-* questions are quite easy to form once you have the correct word order—you just place the question word at the front.

- Next write *Are they in Lima* on the board. Introduce the word *where* and then ask students if they can change the question from a *Yes / No* one to a *Wh-* question. (Have a volunteer come to the board and try it.) Finally, do the same thing on the board with the question *Is she your friend?*

- Have students look at the chart. Point out the Notice! information box to students so that they understand that there are often two ways to answer *Wh-* questions.

**EXPANSION** Have a group of 5–10 students come to the board. Dictate a *Yes / No* question like the ones used earlier (e.g., *Is she your classmate*). Have each student write the question on the board. Then ask them to make it into a *Wh-* question (e.g., *Who is your classmate?*) Call on a student who is observing (i.e., not at the board) to answer the question. Rotate so that each student gets at least one opportunity to write on the board.

**SUPPORT** Keep the three question words *who, what,* and *where* written on the board while students are working. Also, for the first couple of rounds, tell students which question word to use if they need the extra support.

**B** 🔊 Track 34 PRONUNCIATION Read the sentences. Then listen and repeat.

- Play the audio and have students listen. The second time you play it, have them listen and repeat.

**LANGUAGE NOTE** As a general rule, *Yes / No* questions have rising intonation at the end (shown by the ↗ symbol) and *Wh-* questions have falling intonation (shown by the ↘ symbol).

**NOTICE** 1. Some students will be less comfortable with intonation patterns and gravitate towards speaking in a monotone. 2. Explain to students that rising intonation at the end of a sentence can signal uncertainty or make you sound less assertive. At this level, it's important for students to try to say the *Wh-* questions with falling intonation in order to make themselves clearly understood.

- After students have listened to the audio, call on different students to say the questions (in random order). For example, if you call out *number 1*, the student will say *Is it a computer?* or *What is it?* as he or she points at something. That same student should then choose a classmate to answer the question.

**LANGUAGE NOTE** 1. *What*, *where*, and *who* can usually be contracted with *is* (e.g., *What's your name? Where's the ATM? Who's she?*), but sometimes in shorter sentences we cannot use the contracted form in writing or speaking: *What's it?* 2. Note that in contractions with *are*, students may hear these forms spoken (e.g., *Who're you? Where're your friends?*) but the full forms should always be used in writing (e.g., *Who are you? Where are your friends?*)

**C** Match the questions and answers.

- In this exercise, students should match the *Wh-* questions on the left with their answers on the right. (Note that some of the answers are "full forms" while others are "short answers.") Ask students to read through all of the questions on the left and make sure they understand the meaning. Explain *job* as necessary. Then do the first item together to show how the exercise works.

- Give students time to do the exercise and check their answers with a partner. Then go over the answers together as a class.

**CHALLENGE** Students should close their books as you will be turning this into a listening exercise.

**PREP WORK** Write the responses to the questions (items a–h in the right hand column) on the board ahead of time. Tell each student (or team of students) that they will have five seconds to choose the correct answer to your question from the list on the board. Go to the first student and read the first question (*Where are you now?*) If the student chooses *b* or *c*, then that's correct and you erase the answer from the board. If the time runs out, go to the next student and ask a different question and see if that student can come up with the answer in five seconds. As each question gets answered and the list of responses gets smaller, the activity should become easier. Keep going until all of the questions have been answered.

**EXPANSION** Have students get into pairs and ask and answer the questions with a partner.

They should give answers that are true for their real-life situations.

**Answers**
1. b   2. e   3. d   4. f   5. g   6. a   7. c   8. h

**D** Follow the pattern. Write questions.

- For this exercise, students will be using the words in the chart to form both *yes / no* and *wh-* questions. Work through the first item together by showing students how if they take a word from each column (A, B, and C), they will come up with the sentence *Where are the students?* Give students time to work through the exercise. Have them work in pairs if they prefer.

**NOTICE** Items 3–5 (A, B, C, D) and 6–8 (B, C, D, E) follow the same pattern. Explain to students that they need to find three sentences of each pattern and that they can write them down in any order.

**SUPPORT** If necessary, tell students to make *wh-* questions for items 3–5 and *Yes / No* questions for items 6–8, though it's more productive if students discover this on their own.

- Give students time to write and then go over the answers together as a class. Answer any questions that may have come up.

**Answers**
Questions 1–2: Where are the students? / Who are the students?
Questions 3–5: Where is your teacher? / Who is your teacher? / What is your nickname?
Questions 6–8: Is your nickname Lola? / Is your teach[er] Mr. West? / Are the students in class?

**E** Work with a partner. Ask and answer the[] questions in **D**.

- Have students ask and answer the que[stions] with a partner. This is an opportunity f[or] to practice the intonation with these (Help students if they find it hard.) E[ncourage] students to make up answers to th[e open-] ended questions: (e.g., *Where are* They're at home. / They're at th[e]

**F** Track 35 Complete the que[stions] and check your answers.

- Tell students that they are[] conversation between th[e] Anong. Give them one [] lines of the dialogue. T[] books.

- Tell students that it's OK if they don't know the answers perfectly. Then ask them a couple of comprehension questions like these:

  *Who are Celia, Lynn, and Anong?*
  *(They are students.)*
  *Who is Anong? (She is a new student.)*
  *Where is she from? (She's from Thailand.)*

- Another option would be to give True-False statements to test comprehension:

  *Celia, Lynn, and Anong are classmates. (True.)*
  *Celia and Anong are old friends. (False.)*
  *Celia is from Thailand. (False.)*

- Once students understand the context for the conversation (one classmate introducing a new student to a third classmate), have them read through the dialogue and predict the answers. Encourage them to use contracted forms of the question word + *be* where possible. Then play the audio and have students check their answers.

### Answers
Celia: Hey, Lynn. It's nice to see you. <u>Who's</u> your friend?
Lynn: Celia, this is Anong. She's our new classmate.
Celia: Hi, Anong. <u>Where are</u> you from?
Anong: I'm from Thailand.
Celia: <u>Are you</u> from Bangkok?
Anong: No, I'm not. I'm from a small city, Chiang Rai.
<u>here are you from</u>, Celia?
· I'm from Brazil.
<u>Where</u> in Brazil?
Sao Paulo.
's nice to meet you, Celia…Hey, <u>is</u> our class

in Room 10.
teacher?

themselves and one student to take on his or her identity as the new student. Together, the three students should come up with a conversation similar to the one in **F** and practice it. Have them change roles and practice again.

**CLASSROOM MANAGEMENT** If there isn't time for students to write out dialogues, you can give them a conversation with the following information removed.

(A) _____: Hey, it's nice to see you. _____'s your friend?

(B) _____: This is (C) _____. She's our new classmate.

(A) _____: Hi! _____ are you from?

(C) _____: I'm from _____.

(A) _____: Are you from _____?

(C) _____ No, I'm not. I'm from a _____ city, _____. _____ are you from?

(A) _____: I'm from _____.

(C) _____: Where in _____?

(A) _____: From _____.

(C) _____: Well, it's nice to meet you. Hey, is our class in Room 15?

(B) _____: No, today it's in Room 10.

(C) _____: OK. _____'s our teacher?

(B) _____: Ms. Lopez.

(C) _____: OK, thanks. Bye.

(A) _____ & (B) _____: Bye.

- For the first round, you should walk through how to fill this in with students. Tell them that the students who are playing the parts of Celia (A) and Lynn (B) should fill in the (A) and (B) blanks with their own (real) names. The student who is playing the part of the new student, Anong (C), should fill in his or her new name that he/she created in **G**.

  *er students have filled in all of the (A), (B), and ) blanks with their names, Students (A) and (C) have a few more blanks to fill in with country and city names as well as *wh-* question words. (Refer students to the original conversation in **F** if they are not sure what goes in a particular blank, but have them try to do the activity first without looking.)

- Once students have constructed their original conversations, give them some time to practice. If you have time, you can have the students fill out one or two more versions of these conversations so that other students get a chance to play the "newcomer" role in the dialogue.

**EXPANSION** Have some groups perform their conversations in front of the class. Remember, the performances don't have to be perfect. Encourage students to relax and have fun with it.

# 2 SEE IT AND SAY IT

**A** Look at the information. Use *there is / there are* and the words in the box. Write sentences.

- Have students look at the picture and say where it is. Point out the airport arrivals board. Explain what the word *flight* means and call on individual students to read the different flight numbers in English. Tell students what the word *from* means and have individual students read the names of the cities on the arrivals board aloud.

- Demonstrate how the exercise works by going through the first item together. Review the grammar by putting the following on the board:
  _____ a / one flight from La Paz.
  _____ no / two / some flights from La Paz.

- Ask students to tell you which sentence takes *There's* and which one takes *There are*. Remind students that in this exercise, when there is only one flight from a particular city, they can use *a* or *one* in their answer; both are acceptable.

- Give students time to work and then go over the answers as a class.

**CLASSROOM MANAGEMENT** If time is short, put students in pairs and have them discuss the answers without writing anything down. Come back together and review the answers verbally. If you want students to get writing practice, you can assign the exercise as homework.

**B** 🔁 Complete the chart. Use the model. Say sentences about cities and people.

- Give students time to complete the chart. They should work individually and then compare their answers with a partner by saying their sentences to each other. Have individual students tell you about the different cities and people.

**PREP WORK** Enlarge a copy of the chart and tape it to the board at the front of the room or project the chart onto the wall. Call on individual students to come to the chart, choose any empty spot in it, and fill in the answer. (If you are projecting onto a wall, you can call on students to pick an empty cell and spell out the missing word while you write it in.) After the word has been entered, you can ask the class if it's been spelled correctly or not.

- Another way to make this interesting that requires less prep work is to have students work in pairs and ask each other for the answers. Taking turns, students ask each other questions like this:

  A: What's the answer here? (pointing to space on chart)

  B: It's Mexican.

  A: Can you spell that, please?

  B: Sure. It's M-E-X-I-C-A-N.

**C** Choose a city in **B**. Write four sentences about it in your notebook. Use these words.

- Say the words in the box and have students repeat them. Then have students write about the city they chose. Monitor and provide help as necessary. Write any other vocabulary students ask for on the board so everyone can see it.

**D** 🔁 Tell a partner about your city.

- Model the activity by telling students about your city using some of the words in the box. Then assign students to pairs to talk about the cities they chose.

# 3 IS THERE A CAFE AROUND HERE?

In this activity, students will review asking for and giving directions. They will ask each other questions to find missing information on their maps.

**A** 🔁 Work with a partner.
**STUDENT A:** Look at this page.
**STUDENT B:** Turn to page 103.

- Before students do this activity, have them turn to pages 34–35 to review the ways of asking for and giving directions.

- Then put students in pairs. Student A should look at page 45 and Student B should turn to page 103. On their respective pages, have students read directions and the sample dialogue (*Excuse me. Is there a…*) and study their maps silently. Then model the activity with a volunteer.

- Student A begins by asking about one of the places listed (e.g., *Excuse me. Is there a cafe around here?*).

- Student B should locate the place on his map and give Student A directions to it from the "You are here" point on the map (e.g., *Yes, go straight and…*).

- Student A should follow the directions from the "You are here" point, and write the place on one of the white cubes on his or her map.

**NOTICE** If Student A asks about a place that is not on Student B's map (e.g., *Is there a gym around here?*), Student B should say *Sorry, I don't know.*

Then Student A should write an X on that word. Make sure that you model one of these examples with the class.

**SUPPORT** Tell students they will label four places on their maps. They will write an X on two words.

**CHALLENGE** Have students cover the model dialogue near Exercise A as they ask for and give directions.

- After Student A is done asking about all six places, it is Student B's turn to ask for directions to six different places. Student A should listen and give Student B directions.

- After Student B is done asking about the six places, students should show each other their maps and check each other's answers.

**Answers**

On the map, Student A labels *a cafe, a subway station, a post office, a supermarket* and puts an X on the words *a gym* and *a gas station*.

On the map, Student B labels *a bus stop, a Chinese restaurant, an ATM, a bookstore* and puts an X on the words *a drugstore* and *a parking garage*.

# 7 FAMILY

## 1 VOCABULARY

In this Vocabulary lesson, students will learn to talk about members of their family.

**A** 🔊 **Track 36** Find Zoe on page 46. Then listen and say the words (1–11) in the box.

- Before students listen to the audio, do the following:
- Point to the family tree and say to students *They are a family.* Make sure that students understand the meaning of the word *family.*
- Then have students find Zoe (pronounced *Zō-ee*) in the family tree. Point to her picture and say to students *This is her family.*
- Next, have students look at the list of words (1–11) in the box (*grandmother, grandfather, mother*). These are the words Zoe uses to refer to the people in her family. Tell students to match a word in the box with a photo on the page. Do a couple to get them started: Point to Zoe and then Diana and say *her grandmother.* Point to Kevin and say *her grandfather.* Give students a few minutes to match each word in the box to a photo silently on their own.
- Play the audio. As the speaker says a word, students should repeat it and point to the person or people on the page.

> **LANGUAGE NOTE** After you listen to the audio, look at Marisa and Dylan. Write the following on the board:
>
> *Zoe is 16.*
>
> *Marisa is 19. Marisa is her <u>older</u> sister.*
>
> *Dylan is 13. Dylan is her <u>younger</u> brother.*

(Note: Saying one's age will come up later in the unit. For now, just use the numbers in the sentences to illustrate the meaning of the words *older* and *younger.*)

> **LANGUAGE NOTE** CULTURE Point out that *mom* and *dad* are commonly used, informal ways of talking to or about one's mother and father. (Very young children may use *mommy* and *daddy.*)

**EXPANSION** Tell students to take three small slips of paper. On one, they should write *woman,* on another *man,* and on a third *both.* Then call out a new vocabulary item from page 46. If it's a word used to describe a man (*brother, father, grandfather, uncle*), students should hold up the word *man.* If it's a word used to describe a woman (*sister, mother, grandmother, aunt*), students should hold up the word *woman.* If it's a word that can be used to describe both men and women (*parents, grandparents, cousin*), students should hold up *both.* Do this with the class with all of the new words. Then have students do the exercise in small groups for additional practice.

**B** Complete the sentences about Zoe's family.

- In this exercise, students will talk about how the people in the family tree are related to Zoe. Direct students to sentence 1 and do it with the class.

> **LANGUAGE NOTE** POSSESSIVES Point out the Notice! information. In English, there are different ways of talking about ownership. One way is using possessive adjectives (which students saw in Unit 4): *This is <u>my</u> family.*
>
> Another way is by adding an apostrophe + s ('s) to a noun.
>
> *Dylan is <u>Zoe's</u> brother.* (This sentence means *Dylan is her brother.*)
> *Her <u>sister's</u> name is Marisa.*
> With plural nouns (e.g., *parents*), add only an apostrophe (') after the s.
> *Her <u>parents'</u> names are Teresa and Paul.*

Students will not be asked to use possessive nouns in this unit, only recognize them.

- Before students complete sentences 2-11, say each family member's name aloud to ensure that students can pronounce them. Two that may be harder to sound out from the spelling are Zoe (pronounced *Zō-ee*) and Dylan (*Dil-lun*). Then do the following:

- Complete sentence 2 with students.

- Have students complete sentences 3-11 on their own or with a partner.

- Then have them take turns saying the sentences aloud with a partner.

**Answers**
1. (younger) brother   2. father / dad   3. (older) sister
4. mother / mom   5. uncle   6. grandmother
7. cousin   8. aunt   9. grandfather   10. parents
11. grandparents

**EXPANSION** Tell students to take a piece of paper and number it 1–11. Then have them cover the word list and their answers in **B**. Say to them: *Look at Zoe.* Then dictate an incomplete sentence from **B** to the class (e.g., *Marisa is her…*). Students should look at the family tree and write the correct answer (e.g., *older sister*). Do the same with the rest of the sentences, but mix them up so they are not in the same order as in **B**. At the end, check answers.

**C** 🔁 Work with a partner. Look at the pictures on page 46.

- Cover the word list and your answers in **B**.

- Say a sentence about each person in Zoe's family.

- Have students cover the word list and their answers in **B**. In pairs, they should look at the family tree and take turns saying a sentence that explains how each person is related to Zoe (e.g., *Dylan is her younger brother.*).

**EXPANSION** Come up with 8-10 different sentences about the family pictured, similar to those in **B**, using only the new vocabulary. For example:

1. Look at Lucas. Teresa is his _____.

2. Look at Dylan.  Kevin and Diana are his _____.

3. Look at Stefani. Diana is her _____.

4. Look at Marisa. Dylan is her _____.

5. Look at Paul and Stefani. Kevin is their _____.

Then do the following:

- Post sheets of paper around the classroom. Next to each sheet, tape a copy of the family tree on page 46 *without* the new vocabulary. (Another option: project the family tree where all students can see it easily.)

- Put students into teams of 3–4 people. Have each team line up in front of a sheet of paper, with the first person in line standing in front of the paper with a pen.

- Tell the student standing at the paper to write the number 1. Then call out your first incomplete sentence (e.g., *Look at Lucas. Teresa is his…*). Repeat the sentence once if needed. The students standing in front of the paper should look at the family tree and write their answer (which in this case would be *aunt*). Give students 20 seconds.

- Read the same sentence aloud again (e.g., *Look at Lucas. Teresa is his…*), and check answers. If a student wrote the correct answer, his or her team gets a point.

- That student then moves to the end of the line. The next student moves forward, writes the number 2 on the paper, and listens and writes the next answer.

- At the end, the team with the most points wins.

- For extra practice, mix up the sentences and play again.

**D** 🔁 Work with a partner. Complete each sentence.

- Have students look at the pictures and complete each sentence with a partner. Check answers as a class.

**LANGUAGE NOTE**   In sentence 3, point out how the pronoun *me* can be used to refer to oneself: *This is me and my dad. This is my dad and me.*

**Answers**
1. c   2. b   3. b

**E** Find three photos of family members. Write a sentence about each photo in your notebook.

- Many students will have photos on their phones of their family members. Have students find three different pictures (ideally of different family members) and write sentences like those in **D**, describing the people in the photos (*This is my…, These are my…, This is me and…*).

- Help students as needed with the demonstrative pronouns used to talk about the photos: <u>These</u> are my sisters. <u>This</u> is my dad.

**ADDITIONAL VOCABULARY** To talk about their photos, students may need additional vocabulary, for example: *husband, wife, (grand) son, (grand)daughter, niece, nephew, brother-in-law, sister-in-law, mother-in-law, father-in-law.* Circulate and help students as necessary, and put all new words on the board for everyone to be able to use them.

**CLASSROOM MANAGEMENT** If students don't have any family photos on their phone (or don't have a phone), they can do one of the following in **E** & **F**:

1. Tell them to draw their own family tree and then explain it.

2. Tell students to find a photo of a famous family or draw a famous family's tree, and then talk about the people. It can be a real or fictional family (such as one of the families from *Game of Thrones* or the Skywalker family from the *Star Wars* series).

**F** 🔁 Work with a partner. Show and talk about your photos.

- On the board, write things people can say in response to seeing a photo: *Great / nice / cool / cute photo!* Then have students look at the sample on the page and say: *This is my baby cousin, Bella!* Ask the class to use one of the expressions on the board in response (e.g., *Cute photo!*). If you have a family photo, show it to students. Tell them to use one of the expressions on the board in response.

- Then, put students in pairs and have them show and talk about their photos. Remind them to use the expressions on the board in response to seeing a photo.

**CHALLENGE** Tell students to show their photo to a partner without explaining it. Their partner should guess who's in the picture by pointing and asking questions: *Is this your older sister? Are these your parents?*

**G** 🔁 Repeat **F** with a different partner.

- Have students repeat **F** with three or four more people. At the end, poll the class to see which family members were mentioned most often.

# 2 GRAMMAR

This Grammar lesson will introduce the irregular verb *have* (only in the affirmative) and contrast it with usage of the verb *be* (which students have already learned).

**A** Study the pictures and the chart.

- Note: Although students have already learned verbs other than *be* in this course, they have encountered them only in the imperative form (*write your name*), not in their conjugated form with subject pronouns (*I write, she writes,* etc.). Here, students will be seeing *have* in the affirmative only and comparing its usage to the verb *be*.

**LANGUAGE NOTE** *Have*, when used as a main verb, is used in different ways:

1. to talk about possession: *They have a new car*.

2. to talk about personal characteristics: *She has long hair*.

3. to describe relationships: *I have a brother and two sisters*.

4. to describe certain actions: *have breakfast, have a lot of homework, have free time*

- Have students look at the first photo as you read the first sentences from the chart (*I have a big family / You have a big family*) together. Do the same with the other two photos as well. Pay attention to the rhythm and stress of the sentences.

- Now tell your students that you will say some sentences with *have* and they should raise their right hand if they think it's a true statement, left hand if they think it's false, and both hands if they aren't sure. Then say some sentences using a variety of pronouns:

  *They have small families.* (pointing at a group of students)
  *I have long hair.*

  *He has a lot of friends.* (pointing at one student)

**PRONUNCIATION TIP**

Help students notice that both *have* and *has* are pronounced with the /æ/ sound, and that the final *s* in *has* is pronounced /z/, as in *is* /ɪz/.

**B** Circle the correct words.

- Introduce the words in the Word Bank (*free time* and *homework*).

- Have students read through the sentences silently and answer any questions they may have about vocabulary. Go over the first sentence together and make sure students understand the answer. Then give them some time to do the exercise themselves.

- Go over the answers as a class. A fun way to do this is by having students tilt their heads to the right for *have* and to the left for *has*. Read the sentences in unison, and when they get to the words *have* or *has,* students should move their heads in the appropriate direction at the same time. This can be quite amusing and will quickly show you which answers students may not understand.

**EXPANSION** Have students rewrite the sentences to make statements about their own lives or about people they know. For example, for item 1, a student might say *Graciela always has fun in class.* The important thing in this case is that they change *have* from the original sentence (*I have…*) to *has.* If they get stuck on one particular sentence, they can make something up. For item number 6, give them this structure:

The _____ family **has/have** ___ children.

Give students time to write and then go over the answers as a class.

**CLASSROOM MANAGEMENT** If time is short, rather than having students write out their sentences, ask students to volunteer answers orally. They can do the written work as homework. Another option is to tell students to pick one or two sentences to rewrite (not all eight) and then call on some students to give their answers. Tell them they can finish writing out the remaining sentences as homework.

**Answers**
1. have   2. has   3. have   4. has   5. has
6. have   7. has   8. have

**C** 🔊 Track 37 Listen. Say the numbers.

- Play the audio and have students follow along in their books with their fingers as they listen. Play the audio again and have them listen and repeat.

- Explain that although the numbers from 40–100 are not all written out, they follow the same pattern as what's presented from 21–40 (e.g., *forty-one* is followed by *forty-two,* then *forty-three*). Say the numbers from 40–50 as students

listen and repeat. Then go around the room with each student saying a number from 51 on, until you reach 100. Let students know we often say *a hundred* rather than *one hundred.*

- Spend some time focusing on the pronunciation of 13 (thirTEEN) and 30 (THIRty) and other similar pairs. Students can tap the accented syllable in each word as they hear or say it.

- Write the following pairs of numbers on the board: 13/30   14/40   15/50   16/60   17/70   18/80   19/90

- Tell students to choose five of these numbers at random and write them on a piece of paper. Then have students get into pairs, sit back to back, and take turns reading a number from their list. Students who are listening should write down the numbers they hear, and when the activity is finished, have the students compare their lists of numbers to see how they did.

**D** 🔊 Track 38 Practice saying the numbers. Then listen and repeat.

- Practice saying the numbers together. Then play the audio and have students listen and repeat.

**EXPANSION** Have two students at a time come to the front near the board. When you say a number aloud (any number from 0-100), the first student to rush to the board and write the number correctly wins. That student remains in front of the class and the other student sits down as a new challenger comes to the front.

**E** Read about Mimi. Complete the sentences with *am / is / are* or *have / has.*

- Tell students that they are going to read about a woman named Mimi. First review vocabulary that they have learned (e.g., *job, doctor,* and *home*). Introduce new vocabulary (such as *husband* and *bridge*). Also, draw students' attention to the Notice! note and point out that when we state our age, we say *I am 17 (years old). My brother is twenty-two. My parents are fifty.* Asking for and giving one's age will be practiced in more detail in the Speaking lesson.

- Give students a minute or so (with pens/pencils down) to scan the paragraph silently. Then tell them you are going to do this as a timed activity. Set the time and then give students time to work. (Two minutes should be enough.) Call time and then go over the answers as a class. (It's OK if some students don't finish.) Call on individual students to read a sentence at a time.

**CHALLENGE** After the activity is finished, ask students to talk about an aunt or uncle (or anyone else in their life) using the sentence patterns in **E**. Have them substitute personal information from their own lives (e.g., *I am Dominican and my uncle is Dominican. His name is… He has short hair. He is… years old.*). Model this by talking about someone in your family.

**Answers**
1. am  2. is  3. is  4. has  5. is  6. has  7. is  8. has
9. is  10. have  11. are  12. are  13. have  14. is  15. has

**F** Read the sentences about a young woman, Lourdes Leon, and her famous mother. Complete them with *is / are* or *have / has*.

- Explain to students that they are going to read and complete sentences about a very famous mother and her daughter.

**NOTICE** Don't say much more than that to avoid giving away the answer to this guessing activity.

**PREP WORK** Bring in a picture of Lourdes Leon to show students: *This is a picture of Lourdes, the daughter. Her mother is very famous.*

**CULTURE NOTE** Lourdes Leon (born 1996) is the oldest daughter of the singer Madonna. She has done some work as a model and currently is studying in college. Madonna (born 1958) is the second best-selling artist of all time (following the Beatles) and her albums and live concerts continue to sell well. She has been in the public eye since 1982.

- Give students time to read through the sentences and fill in the missing words. Circulate and assist as necessary.

**LANGUAGE NOTE** Note the use of the word *around* to talk about someone's age when we don't know it exactly. In this case, we can say that Madonna is *around 60 years old.*

**Answers**
1. is  2. is  3. has  4. is  5. have  6. are  7. is
8. has  9. is  10. is

**G** Work with a partner Check your answers in **F**. Then guess.

- Have students get into pairs and go over their answers. Based on the clues, they should then guess the name of Lourdes' famous mother.

**Answer**
Madonna

**H** Think of a person from a famous family. Write sentences about the person in the chart.

- To demonstrate to students how this will work, put the following chart on the board and have students help you fill it in with information about Lourdes Leon. (You may have to fill in some of the information that students don't know.)

| Name of person: *Lourdes Leon* | |
|---|---|
| **From** | *She's from the United States.* |
| **Age** | *She's around 20.* |
| **Appearance** | *She has long hair.* *She's pretty.* |
| **Job** | *She's a student.* |
| **Family** | *Madonna is her mom.* *She has a younger brother. His name is Rocco Ritchie.* |

**CHALLENGE** Before students start the activity, you may want to give them some more vocabulary for describing appearance:

*She has glasses. She's pretty. / He has a beard. He's handsome.*

*She's tall. / He has black hair.*

- Give students time to think of a person. As they fill their charts in, circulate and help with any vocabulary around appearance, jobs, or family. Put any new words on the board.

**I** Tell a partner about your person. Don't say the name! Your partner guesses.

- Students should get together with a partner and take turns reading a clue about their person while their partner guesses. Students can play several rounds of this guessing game by switching partners for each round.

- One way to make the activity more interesting is to create a point system. Have Student A first read all of his/her sentences one at a time while Student B makes a guess after each sentence is read. If Student B guesses correctly after the first sentence, he/she receives 10 points, the second sentence 9 points, and so on. The round ends when Student B guesses correctly or there are no more sentences to be read. For the next round, Student B will read clues and Student A will guess. Students should keep track of their point totals and the winner after several rounds (played with a different partner each time) wins.

# 3 SPEAKING

In this Speaking lesson, students will practice describing appearance, asking about a person's age, and talking about family photos.

**A** Say the sentences in the Useful Language box with your teacher.

- Focus first on the language for describing appearance.

- Have students look at the photo and describe the two men's appearance using *have* in as much detail as they can.

- Then write *He looks like him.* on the board and point to the people in the photo. Explain that we use *look like (someone)* to talk about people with a similar appearance, like the two men in the photo. Then ask students to guess: *Are they brothers?*

- If possible, show a photo of someone in your family you look like. Write *I look like _____.* on the board and complete it for yourself. (Make sure students notice that the verb is now *look*, not *looks*.) Then ask different students to complete the sentence. They can talk about who they resemble in their family (e.g., *I look like my mom.*), or they can compare themselves to someone famous. Summarize their answers for the class by pointing to different students and saying: *You look like...*

- Focus next on asking about age.

- Remind students that they learned numbers 21-100 and saying one's age in the Grammar lesson. Go over the language about age in the Useful Language box with the class. (Asking *how old are you / how old is he* will be new for students.)

- For additional practice, write a name and number on the board (e.g., *mom / 53*). Then ask a student: *How old is your mom?* The student should use the number to answer (*She's fifty-three.*). Then, put up a different name and a number (e.g., *sister / 21*).

Tell the student to ask the question, and point to a different student to answer. Continue doing this with different names and numbers a few more times to give students practice asking and answering questions about age.

- Finally, point to the two men in the photo again. Ask students to guess: *How old are they?*

**CULTURE NOTE** ASKING ABOUT AGE  In a social or business setting, asking a person that you don't know well the question *How old are you?* can seem impolite, especially if the person is older.

**B** 🔊 Track 39  Read and listen to the conversation.

- Have students read the dialogue. Point out that "Colin" (one of the speakers in the dialogue) is one of the men in the photo. Then play the audio once through. For additional practice, play the dialogue again. At the end, ask students the same questions about the two men that you did previously (before students heard the conversation): *Are they brothers? How old are they?*

**C** 🔁 Work with a partner. Say the conversation in **B**.

- Have students work in pairs to practice the conversation in **B**. After they've done it once, have them change roles and practice again.

**D** 🔊 Track 40  Listen. Write the words and numbers.

- Tell students to read the two short conversations to themselves. Then play the audio. Students should write the correct words and ages. Play the audio again if needed.

**Answers**
1A: mom    1B: aunt, 24    1A: her    2A: dad
2B: grandfather    2A: he    2B: 70

**E** 🔁 Work with a partner. Say the conversations in **D**.

- Have students practice saying each conversation in **D** with their partner. Note for students that *Yeah, I know.* (used in Conversation 1) means *Yes, I agree with you.*

**F** Find a family photo on your phone. Complete the sentences.

- Have students look at the photo of the couple in Paris and read the example sentence. Make sure they understand the meaning of the word *wife* (if they haven't already learned it). Then point to the photo and say: *This is my brother. Who is the woman?* (Answer: *his wife*). Then ask: *Where are they?* (Answer: *on vacation in Paris*). Make sure that students understand the meaning of the phrase *on vacation.*

**PRONUNCIATION TIP**

Model the pronunciation of *vacation* for students /veɪˈkeɪ·ʃən/. Point out that the ending *-tion* is always pronouced /ʃən/.

- Then have students work on their own to find a family photo. The photo can be of the student with a family member, or simply other family members (e.g., a photo of a grandparent, cousin, sibling, spouse, child).

- Students should also note where the people in their photo are. They can select from the places listed on the page (*at home, at school, on vacation*) or write a different option. Remind students that they learned *at home* and *at school* in Unit 5. They also learned about other locations (e.g., *at the park*) in Unit 5. In Unit 6, they learned to use *in* to talk about being in a city or country (e.g., *They're in Paris*).

**PREP WORK** If students don't have any family photos on their phone (or don't have a phone), bring in stock photos or magazines. Have students choose a photo and imagine that the people in the picture are their family members.

**G**  Work in a small group.

1. Show your photo. Say your sentences from **F**.
2. Each person says a sentence or asks a question.

- Have students read the example conversation. Model the exercise once with two student volunteers. You can use the photo and the sample dialogue on the page or show one of your own family photos. Show the photo and say something simple about it. (*This is my cousin and me.*) Then, each student volunteer has to say something about the photo or ask a question (like those in the sample dialogue).

- In addition to the statements and questions in the sample dialogue, brainstorm other things one could say or ask about the people in the photo and put all ideas on the board.

   *What's his/her name?*

   *How old is she?*

   *He / She looks like…*

   *Where is she from?*

   *He's handsome.*

   *She's pretty.*

   *Is he / she single?*

- Then have students work in groups to share their photos.

**EXPANSION** Have students swap their family photo with another person in the group. Each student should then write a caption for the photo related to what he/she learned about the people in the picture and where they are.

**H**  Repeat **G** with a new group.

- Students can repeat **G** with different classmates. This time, have students start off by showing their photo and having their groupmates guess who's in the picture by pointing and asking a question (e.g., *Is that your brother? How old is he…twenty? Is that his girlfriend? Are they in Olympic Park?*).

# 8 MY FAVORITES

## 1 VOCABULARY

In this Vocabulary lesson, students will learn to describe movies, TV shows, and music.

**A** 🔊 **Track 41** Listen and repeat.

- The words in the chart are used to describe movies and TV shows, or to talk about different types of music.

- Say the words *movie, TV show, and music* with the class, and make sure students understand the meanings of these words by giving and then eliciting examples of each one.

- Then play the audio. As the speaker says a word, students should repeat it.

- To help students understand the meaning of each word, have them look at the emoji that goes with it. Act out the words *funny, sad,* and *scary* for students to help get the meaning across. For *popular,* you can explain that if something is popular, many people like it.

**ADDITIONAL VOCABULARY** Other simple words that students could use to describe TV shows or movies include *boring, exciting,* and *interesting.*

- Students may be familiar with some (or all) of the words used to describe types of music (*hip hop, pop*) since these English words are often used in other languages. Note that *dance music* is sometimes referred to as EDM (electronic dance music), and *hip hop* is sometimes referred to as *rap music.*

- To reinforce the meaning of each word, play a clip of each type of music for the class.

- Ask students if they can name other types of music (*jazz, classical, reggaetón, R&B, etc.*), or even other subgenres (e.g., within pop music, you can talk about *J-pop, K-pop, C-pop*). Write all ideas on the board.

**B** Look at the photos on page 52. Complete the sentences (1-8) with a word.

- Before students do the exercise, direct their attention to the Word Bank. You can write sentences like these to help you illustrate the meaning of the words:

1. (*Name of a popular song*) is a popular *song.*

2. (*Name of the artist who sings the song in sentence 1*) is the *singer.*

3. (*Name of a well known band*) is a popular *band/group.*

- Next, have students look at photos 1-8 and just talk about what they see in each with a partner. Then have them work on their own or in pairs to complete the eight sentences. Encourage students to use each word in the chart once only.

**C** 🔊 **Track 42** Listen and check your answers in **B**.

- Play the audio and have students check their answers in **B**.

**Answers**
1. pop   2. rock   3. hip hop   4. dance   5. scary
6. funny   7. sad   8. popular

**LANGUAGE NOTE** In sentence three, the answer is *hip hop singer.* You could also refer to this person as a *hip-hop artist.*

**D** Write the words.

- Have students look at item 1 and make sure they know what to do. Then have them work on their own to unscramble the letters and write each word. Have them check answers with a partner, saying and spelling each word aloud and pointing to the picture (1–8) it corresponds to.

**CHALLENGE** 1. Have students cover the word list; then give students two minutes to complete the exercise. 2. Have students cover the word list and play against a partner to see who can finish first.

**E** Write ideas in your notebook.

- Give students a few minutes to think of a different idea for each item (e.g., a funny TV show, a famous pop singer or band). Students should do this on their own.

**F** 🔁 Work with a partner. Say your ideas in **E**. Are any of your answers the same?

- Have students discuss their ideas from **E** in pairs. If their partner doesn't know a movie, show, song, or musician mentioned, have students use their phones to find a video or song clip to play.

- Have students note which of their answers are the same (e.g., they both say the same TV show). At the end, poll students to see which shows, movies, songs, and musicians were mentioned the most often.

**EXPANSION** Have students pair up with a new partner, but this time have them use their ideas from **E** to play a game of "20 Questions." (You can also limit the game to ten questions, and allow students to give each other hints.)

- Write on the board: *This is a movie / TV show / DJ / singer / song / group.*

- Student A chooses an idea from **E** and then uses the sentence on the board to start (e.g., *This is a singer.*) Student B can then ask up to 20 *yes / no* questions to guess who Student A's singer is. For example:

  A: This is a singer.
  B: Is it a man?
  A: No.
  B: OK, it's a woman. Is she American?
  A: No.
  B: Is she from the UK?
  A: No, New Zealand.
  B: OK, New Zealand. Is she a pop singer?
  A: Yes.
  B: Is her famous song…
  A: Yes.
  B: Is it…

- Model the game once for the class and have them call out *yes / no* questions. See if they can guess the correct answer. Then have students play the game in pairs.

# 2 GRAMMAR

This Grammar lesson will introduce students to regular verbs in both the affirmative and the negative.

**A** Study the charts.

- Note: Although students have already learned verbs other than *be* in this course, they have encountered them only in the imperative form (*write your name*), not in their conjugated form with subject pronouns (*I write, she writes*). They learned the irregular verb *have* in the last lesson, but only in the affirmative. In this lesson, then, students will learn to conjugate several regular verbs in both the affirmative and the negative.

**LANGUAGE NOTE** The simple present tense is used in different ways:

1. to state what is true in the present: *I live in Buenos Aires. She studies English.*

2. to talk about routines or habits: *He watches TV. They read books.*

3. to state facts: *Americans like peanut butter. There are around 130 million people in Mexico.*

4. to talk about schedules in the future: *The store opens at 10:00.*

**NOTICE** This lesson will touch on the first two uses (stating what is true in the present and talking about routines). The last two uses (stating facts and talking about schedules in the future) will not be introduced.

- Read the sentences in the affirmative statements chart while students listen and repeat. What do they notice about the form of the verb? (Answer: In the 3ʳᵈ person singular, with *he* and *she*, you must add the letter *s* to the verb *like*.) Explain that this rule applies to the pronoun *it* as well. (Note that there are some other spelling rules with the 3ʳᵈ person singular that will come up later in this lesson. For now, focus only on adding the letter *s* to the verb.)

- Practice making sentences with the verb *like*. Take a survey by asking students to raise their hands if they like hip hop. Then ask different individual students to make sentences about their peers (*he likes hip hop, they like hip hop,* etc.) Stay with the affirmative structures for the time being. Mix it up by asking students to make sentences about popular singers and songs so that students get more practice with the verb *like*.

**LANGUAGE NOTE** Students will encounter the use of *do* as the main verb in a sentence in Unit 10 (*do homework*). For this lesson, however, they will be learning about the auxiliary (helping) function of the verb *do*. There are two common uses of the auxiliary:

1. in negative sentences: *I don't like hip hop.* (focused on in this lesson)

2. in questions: *Do you like hip hop?* (presented in Put it Together 3, after Unit 9)

This auxiliary usage does not occur with the verb *be* so it will be new to students. They will need time to practice it.

- Work with the sentences in the negative statements chart in the same way as for the affirmative statements. Read through the sentences with students repeating. Again, point out that the 3rd person singular form (*doesn't*) is different from the other form used (*don't*). This time take a poll about what students <u>don't</u> like and have them raise their hands to vote while individual students make sentences (e.g., *We don't like homework, She doesn't like homework*).

**LANGUAGE NOTE** Students may want to put an *s/es* on the verbs for 3rd person singular when using *does/doesn't*. Point out to them that there is an <u>es</u> in *do<u>es</u>* and *do<u>es</u>n't*, so they don't need to mark the verb with *s/es*. Demonstrate this as follows:

1. *He/She like<u>s</u> rap.*

2. *Do<u>es</u> he/she like<u>s</u> rap?*

3. *He/She do<u>es</u>n't like<u>s</u> rap.*

Students may need reminding that they only need the *s/es* in the affirmative.

- Pronunciation point: While the main verb *like* is emphasized in the affirmative sentences, in the negative ones the auxiliary form of *do* (*don't* or *doesn't*) is emphasized.
  *I <u>like</u> hip hop.* vs. *I <u>don't</u> like hip hop.*

**EXPANSION** Ask each student to write one affirmative and one negative sentence about themselves using the verb *like*. Have some students share their sentences with the class.

**B** 🔊 **Track 43** Look at the pictures. Listen and repeat.

- Play the audio while students listen and repeat. Can they come up with any other words that go together with these verbs? (Possible answers: *play soccer, watch TV, read books*). Point out the Notice! information about the use of *watch* rather than *look at*.

**LANGUAGE NOTE** Some spelling rules that apply to verbs in the 3rd person singular are:
<u>Regular</u>: Add an *s* (*like → likes*)
<u>Irregular</u>:

1. For verbs ending in *s/sh/ch/x*, add *es*: (*watch → watches*)

2. For verbs ending in a consonant + *y*, change the *y* to *i* and add *es*: (*study → studies*)

3. For verbs ending in a consonant + *o*, add *es*: (*go → goes*)

For this lesson, students will only encounter verbs that fit under the first two irregular spelling rules. It's useful for students to have all the rules together in general. However, for some students, it may be too much information. Decide which approach is best for your students.

**C** Circle the correct words.

- Ask students to skim the items and make sure they understand all of the vocabulary. Give them time to do the exercise and then go over the answers as a class.

**CLASSROOM MANAGEMENT** If time permits, have individual students come to the board and write out their answers. You can have several students writing the same sentence at the same time on the board to give lots of students writing practice.

**Answers**
1. have   2. like / doesn't   3. plays / play
4. don't / watches   5. reads / read   6. study

**D** 🔊 **Track 44** PRONUNCIATION Read the sentences. Then listen and repeat.

- Before you play the audio track, write all the subject pronouns in a column on the board and the verbs from **A** and **B** (*like, play, watch,* and *read*) on the board. As you point to a different pronoun/verb combination on the board, have students call it out (e.g., *they play, we read, she watches*). Do this several times, making a note of how the students are pronouncing the verbs in the 3rd person singular (with *he, she,* and *it*).

There are three common ways verb endings are pronounced in the 3rd person singular:

1. as an unvoiced /s/ as in *likes*
2. as a voiced /z/ as in *plays*
3. as an extra syllable /ɪz/ as in *watches*

As all of these endings occur frequently, teach all three. The important thing to emphasize is that the third pronunciation requires an additional syllable while the first two don't.

- Play the audio and have students listen and repeat.

**EXPANSION** Give students some other verbs in the 3rd person and pantomime their meaning while students repeat them after you. (Students don't need to write down or even remember these verbs; you are only saying them to give students more practice with the different pronunciation of the verb endings.)

| | | |
|---|---|---|
| *likes* | *plays* | *watches* |
| *drinks* | *reads* | *washes* |
| *sits* | *stands* | *exercises* |

**E** Write true sentences about a friend or a family member. Use the sentences in **C** as a model.

- For this activity, students are going to write about a friend, classmate, sibling, or other relative that they know. They can use the sentences in **C** as a model, but they don't have to follow it exactly. (The important thing is that they get practice writing some sentences in the affirmative as well as the negative.) Depending on the amount of time that you have, set the number of pairs of sentences you want students to write (from 3-6).

- Remember to give them some time to think of a person that they know well. Tell them it should be someone that they know well enough to be able to write about.

- To make this activity more fun, you can give students the option of writing about themselves in comparison to a famous person. Tell them to use their imagination (e.g., *I have a friend. His name is Justin Bieber. We are very different. I like… Justin doesn't like…*).

- At the end of the activity, have individual students share one or two sentences (they don't have to read the whole thing) with the class.

**F** Complete the chart. Write sentences about yourself.

- Students are now going to play a True/False guessing game. For this first part, they are going to write four pairs of sentences about four different topics. (See the example given in the chart.) The True/False sentences can be affirmative/negative statements (e.g., *I have a lot of friends / I don't have a lot of friends*) or they can be sentences where the noun changes in each case: (*I don't like hip hop / I don't like dance music*).

**SUPPORT** For students who are struggling to come up with ideas, tell them they can use some of their ideas from **E** to get started.

- For this activity to work, students must write sentences that are true in their own lives on the left and false sentences on the right. (In other words, one sentence in each row must be true for the student who wrote it.)

**NOTICE** Students should not let any of their classmates see what they are writing.

- Circulate and help with vocabulary as necessary, as students may want to express ideas that they don't have the words for yet. Keep a running list of these new words and after the game is completely finished, you can put them on the board for everyone to see. (Don't do so yet, though, as it could potentially spoil the game for some students.) Make sure everyone has finished writing before you move on to the next step.

**G** Work with a partner. Read a sentence. Your partner guesses true or false. Take turns.

- Model the game with a student by reading two sentences about yourself. If the student guesses correctly write a point for him/her on the board. If not, assign the point to your name on the board. Then put students into pairs. Student A reads one of his/her sentences from the first row in the chart. (It's up to each student whether they choose to read a true statement or a false one.) Student B should then try to guess whether the statement is true or false.

- Student B then reads his/her first sentence while Student A guesses. After they finish the first row, they should continue until all four rows have been completed.

- If a student guesses correctly, he/she receives a point. If he/she isn't correct, the student who read the statement scores a point. At the end of the game, see who in the class scored the most points. (And remember to introduce any new vocabulary that came up during the activity to the class if there is time.)

**H** 🔁 Work with a new partner. Play the game again.

- Assign students to new pairs to play again. If time allows, students can change pairs several times.

# 3 SPEAKING

In this Speaking lesson, students will practice talking about TV shows, movies, and music they like and don't like.

**A** Say the sentences in the Useful Language box with your teacher.

- Have students look at the photo. Point to the TV and ask them: *What's on TV?* (Answer: a soccer game) Then ask: *Do you like soccer?* Before students answer, direct their attention to the expressions in the Useful Langauge box and say them with students, pointing out the meanings of each:

- *Yes, I love it!* means you like something very much.

- *Yeah, it's OK.* means that you like something, though not necessarily a lot. (*OK* is pronounced as the letters *O* and *K*.)

- *No, not really.* means that you don't like something.

- Ask students the question again: *Do you like soccer?* Ask different students for their opinions using the new expressions.

**ADDITIONAL VOCABULARY** If a person really dislikes something, it's also possible to use these stronger expressions: *I can't stand it.* or *I hate it.*

**LANGUAGE NOTE** Note that students have not learned to ask *yes / no* questions with verbs other than *be*. In this speaking lesson, they will learn how to ask and respond to a *yes / no* question with the verb *like* as part of a fixed expression (e.g., *Do yo like...? Yeah, I love it.*). Students will learn how to ask *yes / no* questions with verbs other than *be* (*Do you have class today? Yes, I do. / No, I don't.*) in Put it Together 3, after Unit 9.

**B** 🔊 Track 45 Read and listen to the conversation.

- Have students read the dialogue to themselves silently, and then play the audio once through. Direct students to the photo on the page so that

they understand what *The Walking Dead* refers to. For additional practice, play the audio again.

**LANGUAGE NOTE** In the dialogue, the question *What else?* is short for *What else is on TV?* The phrase *What else* means "what more" or "what extra." The speaker asks the question because he wants to know what other shows are on TV (in addition to soccer).

**CULTURE NOTE** *The Walking Dead* is a TV show about a group of people who are trying to survive in a world that's been taken over by zombies. (A zombie is a dead person who has come back to life.) The show, which is based on a comic book series and first debuted in the US in 2010, is now available in countries all over the world.

**C** 🔁 Complete the sentences with a partner.

- Have students complete sentences 1 and 2 about the dialogue in **B**, and then give their opinion about movies and shows about zombies in sentence 3.

**Answers**
1. Ken, his favorite   2. Matt, scary   3. Answers will vary

**D** 🔁 Say the conversation in **B**.

- Have students work in pairs to practice the conversation in **B**. After they've done it once, have them change roles and practice again.

**EXPANSION** While students are practicing, write the following conversation on the board or project it with half of it missing:

Matt: _____?

Ken: Well, there's a soccer game.

Matt: _____?

Ken: *The Walking Dead* is on. Do you like that show?

Matt: No, _____.

It's scary. _____?

Ken: Yeah, I _____! It's my favorite show.

- Tell students to close their books, look at the conversation on the board (or screen), and using the prompts available, say the conversation again. Can they remember the words? When students are done, invite one pair to come to the front of the class to role play the dialogue (as if they were sitting in front of a TV or computer searching for something to watch).

**E** 🔄 Say the conversation again. This time, talk about a TV show you know. Use the Useful Language box to help you.

- Have students practice the dialogue in **B** again. This time, have them substitute their own ideas.

**F** Look again at **E** on page 53. Write each of your ideas on a small piece of paper.

Model for the class what to do:

- Take eight small slips of paper.
- Look again at **E** on page 53.
- On a slip of paper, write one idea you had in **E**. For example, if your popular TV show idea was *The Walking Dead,* write that on a slip of paper (as shown on page 57). Do the same for the other seven ideas.

**G** 🔵 Work in a small group. Take turns.

1. Put all the papers from **F** together on a desk.
2. One person takes a paper.
3. He or she asks the group a *Do you like…?* question.
4. The other students answer and explain.

- Have students work in small groups and do the following (Model this once for the class.):
- Students should put all of their papers together, shuffle them, and then place them facedown on the desk.
- One person starts by taking a paper and asks the group a *Do you like…?* question as shown in the sample dialogue on the page.
- Each person in the group then gives an opinion. Encourage students to say more than just *Yes, I love it.* or *No, not really.* Tell them to explain by adding one more sentence, as shown in the sample dialogue on the page. (*Yes, I love it. Her music is great.*)
- After everyone in the group answers the question, discard that paper, and then it's another student's turn to take a paper and ask the group a question.
- Point out that if students aren't familiar with a show, movie, song, or singer, they can say *I don't*

*know that song/singer/show/movie.* or *I don't know it.* The other people in the group can then say a bit more. Put some example sentences on the board to help students navigate this situation. For example:

*Do you like the pop song* Hello *by Adele?*

*I don't know that song.*

*Really? (Sings some of the song)*

*Do you like the show* Game of Thrones?

*I don't know it.*

*It's very popular. It's on (name of TV channel). In the show, there's a…*

**CLASSROOM MANAGEMENT** Another way of doing **F** and **G** is as follows:

- Have students work in small groups. Ideally, each group will have the same number of people (i.e., every group will have three students or four students).
- Have each group come up with two *Do you like…?* questions. One should be about TV and movies; the other question should be about music. Students can use the ideas from **E** on page 53 to help them generate their questions.
- Assign each person in a group a letter. So, for example, if there are three people in each group, assign students the letters A, B, and C.
- Then have all student As get together in one group, all student Bs get together in another group, and so on. In their new groups, each student should ask their two questions and record the answers the other people give.
- Students should then return to their original group and share their answers. The group secretary should write a short summary of the results.
- Finally, the group should present their results to another group or the class (e.g., *Ten people in our class love the pop song* Hello. *Eight people don't like it. One person says it's OK.*).

**EXPANSION** For additional practice, or instead of doing **F** and **G**, do the following:

- Put the three questions on the board and tell students to answer them on their own.

1. *What's your favorite song?*
2. *What's your favorite TV show?*
3. *What's your favorite movie?*

- Then have students write their answers on the board under different headers (*favorite song, favorite TV show, favorite movie*), or use an electronic survey or polling tool that will allow you to capture and display/distribute all answers to the class.

- Put students in pairs or small groups. Have them review the class data. Are any songs, TV shows, or movies mentioned several times? Then tell students to answer the following questions (assist with vocabulary as needed):

1a. In this class, what is a popular song?
1b. Who is the singer or band?
1c. Do you like it?

2a. In this class, what is a popular TV show?
2b. Is it a funny / sad / scary show?
2c. Do you like it?

3a. In this class, what is a popular movie?
3b. Is it a funny / sad / scary movie?
3c. Do you like it?

# 9 TIME

## 1 VOCABULARY

In this Vocabulary lesson, students will learn to tell the time in English and talk about their school schedules.

**A** 🔊 Track 46 Listen and repeat.

- Before students listen to the audio, do the following:

- Write the question *What time is it?* on the board. Under the question write *It's...* Then point to the clock in your classroom or hold up your phone with the time displayed and ask *What time is it?* Point to the word *It's...* and see if anyone can say the time in English. Then say the time aloud for students (e.g., *It's 9:10.*).

- Have students look at each clock on page 58 and read the times to themselves silently.

- Then play the audio. As the speaker says a time, students should repeat it. Point out to students that there are two ways to say many times (e.g., *It's three-oh-five.* and *It's five after three.*)

**SUPPORT** If necessary, focus on only one way of saying a given time. For example, have students say only *It's three forty-five.* and not *It's a quarter to four.*

**B** ⚡ Work with a partner. Cover the sentences in **A**.

**STUDENT A:** Point to a clock. Ask the question.

**STUDENT B:** Say the time.

- Say *What time is it?* and have students repeat the question a couple of times so that they're comfortable saying it. Then have students work in pairs. Student A should point to different clocks on page 58 and ask for the time. Student B should cover the sentences below the clocks with a paper or a finger and reply. Student A should check Student B's answers.

**SUPPORT** Allow students to refer to their books during a first round of asking for and giving the time. Then in a second round, have them cover the times.

**C** ⚡ Change roles. Repeat **B**.

- This time, Student B should point to each clock on page 58 and ask Student A for the time.

**D** Draw four different times in your notebook.

- Point out the two additional ways of saying *It's twelve o'clock.* We use *it's noon* when it's twelve o'clock in the afternoon. We use *it's midnight* when it's twelve o'clock at night.

- Then have students draw four different clocks, similar to those in **A**, in their notebooks.

**E** ⚡ Show your clocks to a partner. Ask for the time.

- Have students work in pairs. Student A should point to a clock and ask what time it is, and Student B should answer. For every correct answer, Student B gets a point. If a given time can be said in more than one way and Student B can say both correctly, he or she gets two points. Model this once with the class.

**EXPANSION** Divide the class into teams. For each team, draw a blank analog clock on the board or a piece of paper you post on the wall.

**PREP WORK** Note: If you use paper, you should prepare multiple copies of blank clocks for each team.

- Draw clocks or position the papers around the room in such a way that students won't be able to see what others write. Then do the following:

- Have each team line up in front of their respective clock, with the first person from each team standing at the board with a marker or in front of the paper with a pen.

- Begin the game by calling out a time (e.g., *four forty-five / a quarter to five*). The students at the board should draw the time on the clock. Give them five seconds.

- Read the same time aloud again and check answers. If a student wrote the correct time on the clock, his or her team gets a point.

- That student then moves to the end of the line. The next student moves forward, erases the time on the board (or puts up a new piece of paper), and listens and writes the next answer.

- At the end, the team with the most points wins.

- For more practice, play again, this time with a student volunteer calling out different times.

**F** 🔊 **Track 47** Listen and repeat.

- Before you play the audio, do the following:

- Direct students to the chart and say: *This is a student's schedule. Her name is Maya.* Make sure students understand the word *schedule*. (A schedule is a list of activities and the times you plan to do them.) In the chart, point out the words *today* and *start*. Translate the word *today* into students' native language, if appropriate in your institute, or have them look it up in their dictionaries. (This word will come up again in the Grammar lesson.) To illustrate the meaning of *start,* you can write on the board: *English class: 10:00-11:00.* Under it write *Class starts at 10:00.* (Note: The word *start* will be formally introduced and practiced more in Unit 10.)

- Next, have students look at the classes in the schedule (*science, math, history,* etc.). Give them a minute to read these to themselves silently. Encourage them to use the icons to help them understand what each class is, or tell them to look the words up in their dictionaries. (Note: P.E. is an abbreviation for *physical education.*) Also point out the meanings of the words *break* (a short time when we stop work to rest or eat) and *lunch* (a meal we eat anywhere from noon to 2:00 p.m.).

- Then play the audio. As the speaker says a word, students should repeat it.

**G** 🔊 **Track 48** Listen to Maya's schedule. Write the times in the chart.

- Play the audio and have students write the time that each class or break starts. Have students

compare answers with a partner. You may need to play the audio more than once.

**Answers**
9:00: English   9:55: science   10:50: math
noon/12:00: lunch   1:00: history   1:45: break
2:15: art   3:30: P.E.

**H** 🔁 Work with a partner. Ask and answer questions about Maya's schedule.

- Direct students to the Notice! note on the page. Point out the difference in the two questions.

1. *What time is it?* asks for the time now. You can answer, for example: *(It's) 2:15.*

2. *What time is your class?* asks when something is scheduled to happen. You can answer, for example: *It's at 2:30.* or *At 2:30.* or simply *2:30.*

- Do one example with the class. Then have students work with a partner and take turns asking and answering questions about Maya's schedule.

**I** Make your class schedule for today. Use the words in **F**.

- Have students make a class schedule for themselves. It can be their actual schedule, or they can invent one. Encourage students to use some of the subjects and activities mentioned in **F**. Circulate and provide more vocabulary as necessary, for example, some students who are taking a science class may want to talk specifically about *biology, chemistry,* or *physics*; students taking math might want to talk about *algebra, calculus* or *statistics.* Put all new items on the board.

**J** 🔁 Work with a partner. Tell him / her about your schedule.

- Have students take turns telling a partner about their schedule (e.g., *My English class is at two o'clock.*).

**CHALLENGE** Another way of doing **I** and **J** is as follows:

- Have students create a schedule similar to the one in **F**. On the schedule, they should list only each class or activity, and next to each, a blank space for "start time."

- Have students pair up with a partner. Student A should give his or her schedule to Student B, who should ask when each activity is (e.g., *What time is your English class? What time is your break?*) Student A should say the time and Student B should write it. At the end, Student A should check Student B's answers.

- Then students should change roles and repeat step 2.

## 2 GRAMMAR

This Grammar lesson will introduce questions with *when* and how to respond to them with specific (*at 2:00*) and general (*in the afternoon, today*) information.

**A** 🔊 **Track 49** Look at the pictures. Listen and say the words.

- Ask students to look at the pictures. Then play the audio while students listen and repeat.

**NOTICE** Make sure students notice that the word *evening* is typically pronounced with two syllables, not three.

**PREP WORK** To give students some practice with the vocabulary, write a simple schedule on the board. Write two subjects/classes in each square of the chart. (This is a good opportunity to recycle the vocabulary students have just learned in the Vocabulary lesson.) For example:

|  | today | tomorrow |
|---|---|---|
| morning | 9:00 – English<br>11:15 – math | 10:35 – history<br>11:50 – P.E. |
| afternoon | 1:05 – lunch<br>2:45 – art | 2:00 – science<br>4:30 – study group |

- Ask students *yes/no* questions about the schedule using the words they've just learned: *Is English in the morning?* (yes) *Is lunch after math?* (yes) *Is study group today?* (no). After you've asked several questions, have students get into pairs. Each student should then ask their partner three *yes/no* questions about the schedule.

**B** Study the chart.

**LANGUAGE NOTE** When a person asks a question with *what time,* he/she usually wants to know a specific time (e.g., *at 10:00*). Questions with *when* are a little more vague in meaning; the questioner may be satisfied with an answer of a specific point in time or even a rough approximation of the time (*in the afternoon*). This first chart introduces *when* to students and they can see both general and specific responses. (Students worked with *what time* in the Vocabulary lesson.)

- Read the question and the different responses in the chart. Point out to students that the preposition *at* is used before a specific time, while *in* is used before an expression indicating a duration of time.

**NOTICE** We also say *at night* instead of *in the evening,* but don't introduce that expression to students here because it will confuse them. (It's an exception to the rule of using *at* for a specific point in time.)

- Go around the room asking individual students questions about their schedule with *when* (e.g., *When is math class? When is lunch?*). Next, write the following words on the board: *at, in, before,* and *after.* Continue to ask questions with *when,* but after each question, point to a different word on the board that students have to include in their answer.

**C** Study the schedule. Complete the sentences. Use the words in the box.

- Ask students to look at the picture: *What time is it?* (Answer: *2:15*). Tell them to look at the chart of the afternoon schedule and go over the first item together. Give them time to complete the remaining sentences in the exercise by using the words in the box.

**D** 🔄 Check your answers with a partner. Ask questions.

- Have students go over their answers from **C** together.

**Answers**
1. now   2. before   3. after   4. tomorrow   5. at   6. in

**EXPANSION** Put students into pairs and tell them that they are going to tell their partner about their schedule. Then write these items on the board: *after, 1:00, afternoon, before,* and *morning.*

**PREP WORK** Make copies of the two schedules (versions A and B) below before class.

- Put students into pairs and give one student the version A schedule and the other one the version B schedule. Tell them to show their partners their schedules and take turns asking each other about them. The student who is responding should use one of the words on the board when answering (e.g., *When is math? / It's after English.*).

| Version A | | Version B | |
|---|---|---|---|
| 10:00 | English | 10:00 | history |
| 1:00 | math | 1:00 | lunch |
| 4:00 | art | 4:00 | science |

**E** Read the conversation. Find five more errors. Correct them.

- Give students a minute to read through the conversation silently. Tell them that this is an error correction exercise; they are going to find the mistakes. Point out the example given (in the last sentence of the conversation, the word *now* has been crossed out and the word *tomorrow* has been inserted).

- Have students work on finding the errors and then go over the answers as a class.

- A fun way to go over the answers is to put students into pairs and have them work together to find the five remaining errors. Give them two or three minutes to work and then ask them to put their pens down. Explain that you are now going to read the dialogue aloud as a chain conversation. Call on a pair of students to stand and read the first two lines only of the corrected conversation. So they would say *What time is our lunch break? / It's **at** 12:00.* Write the correction on the board and make sure everyone has understood it. Then call on another pair to read the next two lines of the conversation. Continue in this way until you have finished all eight lines of the dialogue.

**Answers**
A: What time is our lunch break? / B: It's **at** 12:00.
A: Then when **is science class**? / B: It's at 1:00.
A: Oh, so it's **in** the afternoon. / B: Yes, **after** lunch.
A: Got it. What time **is** our test? / B: The test isn't today. It's **tomorrow**.

**F** 🔊 Track 50 Listen to the conversations. Match each one to a picture.

- Ask students to look at the three pictures. Who do they think the people in the photos are? How do they know each other? Where are they? Point out the word *reservation* in the Word Bank.

- Play the audio. For this first listening, students only need to match the conversation to the correct picture. Review the answers as a class.

**Answers**
1. B   2. A   3. C

**G** 🔄 🔊 Track 51 Read the conversations. Listen again. Write the missing words. Then practice the conversations with a partner.

- Ask students to take some time to read through the three conversations. Clarify the meaning of *please come with me* (conversation 1), *good luck* (conversation 2), and *swim practice* (conversation 3).

- Encourage them to write in any of the words that they can guess. Then play the audio and have them listen and write the answers. Go over the answers as a class.

- Put students into pairs and assign each pair one of the conversations. Have them practice the conversation in stages:

1. First, they can read the conversation aloud as they sit facing one another.

2. Next, ask the pairs to practice reading each sentence silently and then looking up and saying the sentence to their partner (without looking down again).

**PREP WORK** While the students are practicing, you should write the first word of each sentence for each dialogue on the board. So, for conversation 1 you would write the following words on the board: *What, 6:00, Are, Yes,* and *Please.* Do the same for the other two conversations.

3. Finally, have the students practice their conversations with a partner with their books closed. They can look up at the words on the board for help if they get stuck at any point.

- Ask some pairs to perform their conversations for the class. They can check the board if they need help when they've forgotten a line.

**CHALLENGE** Erase all the words on the board and have students perform their dialogues from memory!

**Answers**

| Conversation 1 | Conversation 2 | Conversation 3 |
|---|---|---|
| A: <u>What time is</u> your reservation? | A: <u>When</u> is your test? | A: <u>When</u> is swim practice? |
| B: <u>6:00</u>. | B: It's <u>tomorrow</u>. | B: It's <u>after</u> school. |
| A: Are you all here <u>now</u>? | A: <u>What time is it</u> tomorrow? | A: Is it <u>today</u>? |
| B: Yes, we are. | B: It's at <u>10:00</u> in the <u>morning</u>. | B: No, it's tomorrow at <u>4:00</u>. |
| A: Please come with me. | A: Good luck! | A: Thanks. |

**H** Use the words in the box. Complete the sentences to make them true for you.

- Students will be using the words in the box to complete the sentences below. They are making sentences about their own school schedules.

**NOTICE** 1. Students don't have to use each expression in the box once; they can use an expression as many or as few times as they want. It will depend on their own real-life circumstances. For example, a student's "favorite class" and "favorite part of the school day" could both occur "in the morning." 2. Also, make it clear to students that they are not writing down the name of the activity itself; rather, they are thinking of it and writing down when it occurs (e.g., *after school* or *in the morning*) using the words in the box.

- Point to the Word Bank and go over the different collocations with *club* and *practice*.

**ADDITIONAL VOCABULARY** Brainstorm other club and practice activities (such as *debate club* or *choir practice*) that students engage in in your school and put them on the board. There also might be other activities (such as working on the *school newspaper*) that you can add to your list. Spend as much time on this as necessary to help students with language they may not know. They can then pull from these ideas (if they need to) to complete the sentences.

- Give students some time to think and fill in the sentences.

I 🔄 **Ask a partner questions. Guess the answers.**

- Have students get into pairs. They are going to take turns guessing their partner's answers.

- Model the activity with a student. There are two parts to each round of the guessing game:

    In Part 1, Student A will ask Student B a question using the word *when* (e.g., *When is your favorite class?*) Student B will answer with what he or she wrote down in **H** (e.g., *My favorite class is in the afternoon*).

    In Part 2, Student A continues guessing, but can only ask *yes/no* questions. The round finishes when Student A has guessed Student B's answer correctly. Student A receives one point for each question asked. For example, Student A's turn could go something like this:

    A: When is your favorite class?
    B: It's in the afternoon.
    A: Is it music?
    B: No, it's not.
    A: Is it English?
    B: Yes!
    (Student A receives 3 points, one for each question asked.)

- For the next round, Student B guesses in the same way. After each pair has finished, students can rotate and continue playing the game with different partners, keeping track of their point totals as they move about the room. At the end of it all, the student with the lowest point total wins (because he or she asked fewer questions and guessed the answers more quickly).

# 3 SPEAKING

In this Speaking lesson, students will practice making and replying to suggestions and asking about others' schedules.

**A** Say the sentences in the Useful Language box with your teacher.

- Tell students to imagine this situation: Tomorrow, there is a big English/math/science test. Then point to one student. Say: *You want to study with* (name of another student). For example: *Maria, you want to study with Clara.*

- Then direct students to the first sentence in the Useful Language box. Point out that Maria can say this sentence to Clara, *Let's study together.* (*Together* means to do an activity with another person.)

- Write on the board *Let's + verb,* and point out that to suggest an idea, you use *Let's + (base form of the) verb,* as in the first sentence in the chart (*Let's study together.*). Other examples you can share with students using vocabulary they know could include: *Let's watch a movie. Let's play a video game.*

- Direct students to the sentences in the Useful Language box, and point out how a person can say *yes* to a *Let's...* suggestion (*That sounds good.* or just *Sounds good.*) or *no* (*Sorry, I can't.*).

**LANGUAGE NOTE** When we say *no* to a suggestion, it's common to give a short reason explaining why. In the chart, for example, the person says *Sorry, I can't. I have class.*

- Direct students to the Notice! note. Point out that the verb *have/has* is used with different activities. You can show students sentences like these to explain:

    A: Let's study at 2:00.

    B: Sorry, I can't. I have class / have band practice at 2:00.

- Then practice saying the sentences in the chart for making and responding to a suggestion with the class.

- Next, write on the board *Are you free...?* Point out that this is a question we can ask when we want to plan a time to do something with someone. Direct students to the examples in the Useful Language box (*Are you free at 3:30 / later / in the morning?*), and ask the questions with the class.

- Point out the ways of responding and practice saying them with the class.

**B** 🔊 Track 52 Read and listen to the conversation.

- Have students read the dialogue to themselves silently. Then play the audio once through. For additional practice, play the audio again.

**C** 🔁 Answer the questions with a partner.

- Have students answer the questions about the dialogue in **B**.

**Answers**
1. The test is tomorrow   2. At 3:30 (today)

**D** 🔁 Work with a partner. Say the conversation in **B**.

- Have students work in pairs to practice the conversation in **B**. After they've done it once, have them change roles and practice again.

**E** Cover the Useful Language box and the conversation in **B**. Read the conversations below. Guess the missing words.

- Direct students to the Word Bank and introduce *go shopping* (which means "to go to a store and buy something") and *shoes* (pronounced /ʃuː/). You can point to your shoes to illustrate the meaning of the word. Note that the singular form of the word is *shoe;* the plural is *shoes*.

- Then tell students to cover the Useful Language box and the conversation in **B**, modeling this for them so they know what to do. Have students look at the first two lines in conversation 1. Can they guess any of the words? Then tell students to read the two short conversations to themselves and write their answers.

**F** 🔊 Track 53 Listen. Write the words and the times in the conversations in **E**.

- Play the audio. Students should check their answers in **E**, and write the correct words and times.

**Answers**

A: Let's see the new Batman movie <u>today</u>.
B: I <u>can't</u>. I <u>have</u> a lot of homework.
A: Are you <u>free</u> tomorrow?
B: Yeah, <u>in</u> the afternoon.
A: Great. There's a movie at <u>2:45</u>.
B: OK, <u>let's</u> see it then.
A: That sounds <u>good</u>!

A: I need new shoes.
B: Me too. Let's go shopping <u>after</u> school.
A: Sorry, I <u>can't</u>. I <u>have</u> soccer practice.
B: Are you free <u>later</u>?
A: Yeah, at <u>5:30</u>.
B: <u>Let's</u> go shopping then.
A: Sounds <u>good</u>!

**G** 🔁 Work with a partner. Say the conversations in **E**.

- Have students work with their partners to practice saying each conversation in **E**.

**LANGUAGE NOTE** In conversation 2, speaker A says *I need new shoes.* and speaker B responds *Me too.* This is a short way of saying *I need new shoes, too (also).* We use *me too* to express that we share something in common or feel the same as another person, for example:

*I'm a student. / Me too.*
*I have a math test today. / Me too.*
*I have a sister. / Me too.*
*I like scary movies. / Me too.*

**H** Write your schedule for today and tomorrow. List 4–5 activities each day.

- Have students complete the schedule with their plans for today and tomorrow. They should list any classes, extracurricular activities (e.g., sports practice, drama club), appointments, work, or family plans that they have. For example, if a student has swim practice and it starts at 4:00, the student should write that activity in the chart at that time. If students have no plans during a certain hour, they should leave the space blank. For each day, students should list at least four to five activities, even if they have to make some of their schedule up. Tell them not to fill up every space, though, or they won't be able to do **I**. Help students with vocabulary as needed, and write all new language on the board.

**I** 🔁 Find a time to do the activities with a partner.

- Tell students their goal is to find time in both of their schedules to do the three activities listed (study for a test, see a movie, go shopping). Refer students to the sample dialogue on the page, and model the exercise with a student volunteer. Once students have found a convenient time for both of them, they should write the activity in their charts.

**CHALLENGE** Have students sit back to back and pretend that they're calling their partner to schedule a time to do one of the activities. (This will also recycle language students learned in Unit 4 around answering the phone.) Model this once for students so that they know what to do:

*A: Hello?*
*B: Hi, Mario. It's Diego.*
*A: Hi, Diego.*
*B: Hey, are you free today?*
*A: Yeah, in the afternoon. Why?*
*B: Let's study for our history test together.*
*A: Sounds good. When?*
*B: Are you free at…*

# PUT IT TOGETHER 3

## 1 GRAMMAR

This Grammar lesson will introduce *Yes / No* questions with verbs other than *be* and short answers to those questions (*Do you like hip hop? Yes, I do. / No, I don't.*).

**A** Study the chart.

- Before you introduce the question form, it's a good idea to review statement word order. First elicit the subject pronouns from students (*I, you, he, she, it, we, you, they*) and write them on the board. Then have students come up with a sentence for each pronoun and put it on the board (e.g., *I like hip hop. He reads comic books.*). Check the sentences to make sure students are using the correct form for the 3rd person singular. Leave these sentences on the board.

- Remind students that they learned to ask *yes / no* questions with *be,* and write an example or two on the board. (*He is a student.* ➔ *Is he a student?*) Remind them that the subject (He) and the verb (is) change places to form the question. Then tell students that they are going to learn to ask *yes / no* questions with other verbs.

- Look at the chart. Read the statements together. Then go over the statements one by one and read the corresponding question for each one.

**LANGUAGE NOTE** Your students have learned the negative form of the auxiliary *do* in negative statements (e.g. *She doesn't like pop* or *They don't like scary movies*) in Unit 8. Now they are going to learn the affirmative form of *do* as it is used in Yes / No questions and in short responses to Yes / No questions. (Note that students will learn to use *do* as a main verb when they learn the expression *do homework* in Unit 10.)

**LANGUAGE NOTE** There are two main things students need to notice about the *Yes / No* questions. First, to form the question, insert *do* or *does* before the subject and keep the same word order after that. Second, the verb in the 3rd person for statements (e.g., *She likes hip hop*) changes in the question form (e.g., *Does she like hip hop*). There is only one verb form (the base form) used for all subjects.

- Go back to the statements that you wrote on the board and work with each one to turn it into a question. Ask students to dictate the answers to you as you write them on the board.

**B** Write questions.

- Have students read the sentences silently and ask any questions about vocabulary. (They may not know the use of the word *close* that appears in item 4.)

- Because of the prep work done in **A** it should be clear to students how to complete the items in **B**. Go over the first example on the page and then give students time to write out their questions for the remaining items. Go over the answers as a class.

**Answers**
1. Do you have a big family?  2. Does she like her aunt?
3. Does the café close soon?  4. Does he have class now?
5. Do they like English class?  6. Do we have swim practice now?

**C** Write statements and questions. Follow the pattern.

- For this exercise, students will be using the words in the chart to form both statements and *Yes / No* questions. Take a moment to review how this exercise type works by going over the first item together. Make sure students understand *pet.*

- In item number 1, the letters B, D, and E correspond to the columns B, D, and E in the chart above. Students should choose one word from each of those three columns and construct a grammatically correct sentence (which could be a statement or a question). The challenge comes from the fact that the words are mixed up so students will have to figure out which ones to use. In this case, the answer is *He has a pet,* which students can see in their books. Point out the use of appropriate capitalization and punctuation at the end of the sentence.

- Moving on to item number 2, students should then choose one word each from the same three columns to make a sentence.

**SUPPORT** What makes this engaging for students is that they don't know what kind of sentence to make (statement or question) so they really have to concentrate. If students are really struggling, however, you can tell them that items 1-4 are statements and 5-6 are questions.

**CHALLENGE** Turn this into a game. Put students into groups of four. Two students (A and B) will stay in their seats while the other two (C and D) will be stationed at the board. At the count of three, the game will begin. A and B will look at item 2 and figure out the answer (which is *You have a pet*). Once they think they know the answer, they should raise their hands. Student C should then rush over to them, listen to them whisper the answer, and then return to the board to tell D, who will write the sentence on the board. Students should work through all of the items and the first team to have their sentences on the board, spelled and punctuated correctly, are the winners (so it pays to hurry). The key in this game is that students cannot speak, except to whisper the answer to each other! (Also, make sure students rotate and play different roles; Student D can be Student A in the next round, for example).

**Answers**
1. He has a pet.   2. You have a pet.   3. He doesn't have a pet.   4. You don't have a pet.   5. Do you have a pet?   6. Does he have a pet?

**D** Write affirmative statements (+), negative statements (–), and questions (?). Use the words.

- In this exercise, students will get to recycle everything that they have learned thus far about the simple present: how to form affirmative and negative statements as well as *Yes / No* questions.

- Explain the symbols to the students: the + (plus) symbol indicates that they should write a sentence in the affirmative. The – (minus) symbol is used to mark negative statements. And where they see the "?" (question mark), they should write a *Yes / No* question.

**LANGUAGE NOTE** Errors to watch out for: 1. In the affirmative statements, make sure that students are writing the verb in the 3rd person singular correctly (e.g., *The teacher* <u>asks</u> *questions,* not *The teacher ask...*). 2. In negative statements, check to see that students are using the correct form of *do* (*don't* or *doesn't*) and have spelled the contractions correctly. 3. For the questions, make sure students are using the base form of the verb for all persons and the correct form of the auxiliary (*do* or *does*). In all of the sentences, check for capitalization and punctuation.

- Give students time to write out their answers. Have them compare their answers with a partner and then go over the answers as a class.

**CLASSROOM MANAGEMENT** If time is short, put students into pairs and have each pair write out the answers to a set of three questions only. Then review the answers as a class.

**Answers**
1. They study English.   2. They don't study English.
3. Do they study English?   4. The teacher asks questions. 5. The teacher doesn't ask questions.
6. Does the teacher ask questions?   7. Paula listens to music.   8. Paula doesn't listen to music.   9. Does Paula listen to music?   10. I know the answer.   11. I don't know the answer.   12. Do I know the answer?

**E** Study the chart.

- Students have had the opportunity to practice forming *Yes / No* questions. Now they are going to learn how to respond to them with short answers. (They're called "short answers" because it is not necessary to repeat the information in the question when you respond: *Do you study English? / Yes, I do* ~~study English.~~)

- Read through the questions on the left. First, have students listen and repeat. Then have students say the questions themselves. Listen for rising intonation when students say their questions.

**LANGUAGE NOTE** 1. The first thing for students to notice in the short answers is that some pronouns "shift." For example, the question *Do you like math* elicits the answer *Yes, I do.* This is important to be aware of as it will come up in the exercise that follows. 2. Ask students to notice how contractions are used. (Answer: They are used in negative responses but not in the affirmative ones.)

- Go around the room asking individual students *Yes / No* questions in order to elicit short answers. (Mix these up to make it challenging for students.)

*Do they have homework? Does she play video games? Does he have a sister? Do we like English?*

**CHALLENGE** Students previously learned *Yes / No* questions and short answers with the verb *be*. Mix some of these questions in with some of the ones above and see if students can give the correct short answer:
*Are you a student? Am I a teacher? Am I a soccer player? Is his name Flavio? Are we at home?*

**F** 🔊 **Track 54** Circle the correct questions and short answers. Then listen and check your answers.

- For this exercise, students are going to choose the correct question forms and responses. Point out that the questions are above (1a, 2a, 3a) and their responses are below (1b, 2b, 3b). Note: students know the phrase *open your book* but may not be familiar with the use of *open* in 3a.

- Have students work silently. Then play the audio and have them check their answers. As a final step, call on pairs of students and ask one student to read the question while the second student responds.

**Answers**
1a. Do I know you?   1b. Yes, you do.   2a. Do they play video games?   2b. Yes, they do.   3a. Does the store open at 10:00?   3b. No, it doesn't.

**G** Put the words in order. Write questions.

- In this exercise, students will be unscrambling the sentences to make *Yes / No* questions.

**PREP WORK** One way to make this a fun activity is to make copies of the exercise so that you have one piece of paper for every five students. Put students in groups of five and tell them that they are going to race against the other groups. Pass out the papers face down to the first student (Student A) in each group. On the count of three, all Student As should turn over their papers and unscramble the first sentence. Once they have written out the question, they should pass the paper on to Student B, who will then write out the question for item 2. Students should continue passing the paper down the line in this way until the fifth student (Student E) has written question five. Take the finished papers and post them on the board in the order that they were completed. The group that finishes first *and* has written all the questions correctly wins the game.

- After the game, project the five questions on the wall or hand them out to students so that they can copy them into their Student Books. (They can do this for homework if you like.)

**Answers**
1. Do you have a lot of homework?   2. Does your best friend go to your school?   3. Does your teacher answer your questions?   4. Do you have a big family?
5. Do your classmates like English class?

**H** 🔁 Work with a partner. Ask and answer the questions in **G**.

- Students are now going to pair up and ask and answer the questions in **G**. Before starting the activity, explain what the word *busy* (in the speech bubble) means. (A busy person has many things to do.) After students have completed the activity with their partner, ask them to rotate and find a new partner so that they get a chance to ask the questions again. Students can do this for several rounds.

**EXPANSION** Put students into pairs. Designate one student as a TV interviewer and the other student as a celebrity. (The student can choose who he or she wants to be.) Tell the students that the interviewer is going to ask the celebrity some questions. Brainstorm some ideas as a class and then circulate around the room to help students to come up with their own questions. Some ideas:

*Do you like (insert students' city or country name)?*
*Do you have a girlfriend/boyfriend?*
*Do you have a lot of money?*
*Do you live in a big house?*

- Have students write out their questions and practice their dialogues.

**PREP WORK** While they are doing this, use the time to write the following information on the board: *Hi / Good evening, my name is* (TV presenter's name). *And this is* (celebrity's name). *Welcome to our show. I have some questions.*

- Next, have some students come to the front of the room and perform their skit for the class. Point out the language on the board that the interviewer can use to introduce his or her guest. The rest of the class should play the part of the in-studio TV audience and applaud when the guest is first introduced. Encourage the interviewers and celebrities to play their roles enthusiastically, mimicking the behavior of famous people that they see on TV. At the end of each skit, the "audience" should applaud again as the interviewer thanks the guest and the audience.

# 2 SEE IT AND SAY IT

**A** ⚡ Find Luke. Point to each person in his family and tell a partner. Write your answers.

**PREP WORK** Write the following words on the board: *grandmother, grandfather, mother, father, older brother,* and *older sister.* Practice saying the words together as a class. Then write this sentence on the board: *She / He is his ____.* Point to Luke's best friend in the picture and say, *He is his best friend.* (In all of the sentences, *his* refers to *Luke's.*) Tell students that they are going to choose from among the words on the board to identify the different people in the photo. Note: there are two extra words on the board (*grandmother* and *father*) to make it more challenging.

- Put students into pairs. Students should take turns pointing at different people and identifying them (e.g., *He is his grandfather, She is his older sister*), until each student has had a chance to identify each one. Circulate and help as necessary.

- Go over the answers as a class. Give students time to write their answers in their books. (They only need to write the titles—e.g., *older brother*—rather than the full sentences.)

**Answers**
1. grandfather   2. mother   3. (older) sister
4. (older) brother   5. Luke   6. best friend

**B** 🔊 Track 55   Read the conversations. Guess the answers. Then listen and check your answers. Match the people to the conversations.

- Ask students to read the three conversations. They should "pencil in" any answers that they can guess from the context. (They don't have to fill this in completely because they will be listening to it soon. This exercise is just to give them some practice in predicting.)

- Make sure that students are familiar with the vocabulary used in the conversations. (They may not be familiar with the word *difficult,* for example.)

**CULTURE NOTE** In conversation C, *Family Guy* is mentioned. *Family Guy* is a popular sitcom (situation comedy) about the Griffins, a "typical" American family. Although it is animated, the intended audience for the show is adults, not children.

**PREP WORK** Print out an image of *Family Guy* from the Internet and bring it in to class to show your students.

- Play the audio of the three conversations once or twice, giving students time to check their answers.

**EXPANSION** There is a lot of rich language recycled in these conversations, so you may want to give your students some extra practice with them.

**PREP WORK** Write the conversations on the board or project them on the wall. Once students have all the answers, ask them to close their books. Focusing on the board, have them read the conversations together with you. Next, have two students read a conversation (one taking role A and the other role B). Ask other students to read the conversation as well and each time a different pair does it, remove some of the words on the board so that they have to do more and more of it from memory.

- Finally, play the audio again and together as a class say which conversation is being had by which people in the picture.

**Answers**

| Conversation A | Conversation B | Conversation C |
|---|---|---|
| <u>Mother,</u> <u>grandfather</u> | <u>Luke, best friend</u> | <u>Older sister,</u> <u>older brother</u> |
| **A:** What <u>time</u> is it? | **A:** Do you <u>like</u> video games? | **A:** What time is *Family Guy* <u>on</u>? |
| **B:** It's 8:00. | **B:** Yes, I do. | **B:** At 8:30. |
| **A:** Oh, good. *The Voice* is <u>on</u>. | This one is my favorite. It's <u>scary</u>. | **A:** Oh no. It's only 8 PM. No problem. Let's watch it now. |
| **B:** I don't know it. | **A:** Is it difficult? | **B:** I <u>don't</u> like *Family Guy.* It's boring. |
| **A:** It's a show with <u>singers</u>. Watch. | **B:** No, not really. <u>Let's</u> play it! | **A:** I love it! It's <u>funny</u>! |
| **B:** Wow! He's really good! | | |
| **A:** Yeah, and he's only <u>16</u>. | | |

**C** ⚡ Work with a partner. Choose one conversation. Change the blue words. Make your own conversation.

- Ask students to look at the conversations in **B** again. Point out the words in blue. Explain that they are going to work with a partner and make their own conversations modeled on these examples. They should substitute new information for the words in blue and they can change any other language they want to.

- Give pairs time to work together and circulate to assist as necessary. Then have some students perform their conversations for the class.

# 3 ARE YOU FREE AT 2:00?

In this activity, students will review telling time, making and replying to suggestions, and asking about others' schedules.

**A** 🔄 Work with a partner.

**STUDENT A:** Look at this page.
**STUDENT B:** Turn to page 105.

- Put students in pairs. Student A should look at page 67 and Student B should turn to page 105.

- On their respective pages, have students read the directions for **A** and review their schedules silently. Give students a couple of minutes to note which activities are listed and when they are. If students don't recall what a word means or how to say a given time, tell them to look back at Unit 9 for a quick review.

**CULTURE NOTE** Direct students to the Word Bank and make sure they understand *homeroom*. In many elementary and high schools, this is a room where students gather, usually at the start of the school day, to listen to school announcements. In a homeroom, a teacher also checks student attendance.

**CHALLENGE** Have all Student As gather in one area of the classroom, and pair up with each other. Student Bs should do the same. In each pair, one student recites aloud the activities scheduled for today; his or her partner talks about tomorrow. For example, in a pair of Student As, one person talks about today and says *At eight, I'm free. At eight forty-five, I have homeroom. At nine, I have English.* The other person talks about activities

scheduled for tomorrow and says *Tomorrow, I have study group at eight o'clock. I have homeroom at 8:45. I have a doctor's appointment in the afternoon at 5:30.* Then have students change roles so that the person who talked about today's activities now talks about tomorrow's. Have students keep practicing until they can talk about the activities and times in their schedule (for both today and tomorrow) fluently and with confidence. When time is up, have students return to their seats.

**B** You want to add the two activities below to your schedule. When are you free? Think of times.

- Have students read the directions and look at the two activities they want to add to their schedule. At this point, students should only think about possible times they could do each activity and make some notes; they shouldn't write anything in their schedule yet. They'll be trying to find a time to do the two activities together with their partner in **C**.

**C** 🔄 Ask your partner to do the two activities in **B**. Find a good time for both of you. Then write the activities on the schedule above.

- Point out the phrases in the Notice! note. Then model the activity by reading the sample dialogue with a student. Assign students to pairs. Student A begins by asking Student B to do an activity (e.g., *Let's work on our science project today.*). Student B should reply appropriately (e.g., *Sounds good.* or *OK, when?*). The students should then work to find a time that is convenient for them both, and they should write the activity in their schedule.

**NOTICE** Tell students that they should not let their partner see their schedule. Remind students that if their partner suggests a time to do something and they are busy, they must respond appropriately and explain why they have to decline (e.g., *Sorry, I can't. I have my TOEFL class at 2:00.*).

**CHALLENGE** Have students cover the model dialogue near **C** as they make and reply to suggestions.

- After Student A is done suggesting two activities, it's Student B's turn to ask Student A to do two activities (e.g., *Let's go shopping this afternoon.*). Once again, the students should work to find a convenient time for them to do the activities together and write each one in their charts.

**EXPANSION** After students have completed the info-gap activity, you can use their schedules to give them additional practice with present tense *Yes / No* questions and short answers, which they've just learned on pages 64–65.

Write this question stem on the board: *Do you...?* Nearby, write these school activities: *homeroom, English, Science, Math, TOEFL class, Art History, P.E., Soccer practice, Drama club, study group.*

Then tell students (still working in A-B pairs) to choose a school activity on the board and to ask each other about it and their schedules using *Do you...?* questions. To answer, students should refer to their schedules on page 67 or 105. For example:

*Do you have English today?*
*Yes, I do.*
*When? / What time?*
*At nine o'clock. Do you have English today?*
*Yes, at 2:00.*

Remind students that if they both have a class at the same time, they can use *Me too*, which they learned in Unit 9.

*Do you have homeroom in the morning?*
*Yes, I do. At 8:45.*
*Me too.*

This activity can also be done as a class exercise in which the teacher points to a pair, who stand up. The teacher then points to a school activity on the board and the pair has to ask each other about that activity and their schedules using *Do you...?* as in the examples above. Each student pair can get points for...

1. accuracy (using the language correctly).
2. fluency (being able to ask and answer the questions fluidly, without constant hesitation).

**D** Your partner wants to ask you to do two activities. Listen and look at your schedule. Find a good time for both of you. Write each activity on your schedule.

- Have students switch roles and repeat the activity. Tell students to choose another activity and check their schedules.

# 10 MY ROUTINE

## 1 VOCABULARY

In this Vocabulary lesson, students will learn to talk about activities they do regularly.

**A** 🔊 Track 56 Listen and repeat.

- Before students listen to the audio, do the following:

- Have students look at the photo and then say the title of the unit aloud with you. Explain that a "routine" is a list of activities (like those pictured on page 68) that you do often.

- Have students look at each activity on page 68, and read the words to themselves silently.

**LANGUAGE NOTE** Draw students' attention to the familiar words in **A**. For example, they learned *school* in Unit 5 (e.g., *Maria is at school. There's a school on my street.*). Now they're going to see how this word can be used with the verbs *go (to), start* and *finish*. Students also saw *(have) homework* in Unit 7, and now they will learn to use the verb *do* with the word.

- Then play the audio. As the speaker says an activity, students should repeat it.

- After students say the new vocabulary, help them notice the points mentioned in the language note below.

**LANGUAGE NOTE** MULTI-WORD EXPRESSIONS

1. Many of the activities on page 68 use two or more words to describe an action (*get up, take a shower, do homework, go to bed*). Point out to students that the first word in each phrase changes in the third person (e.g., *I take a shower in the morning. My brother takes a shower in the evening.*).

2. Three of the activities use *go*. Get students to notice the patterns:

   **go to + noun**: *go to school, go to bed*: This is the "regular" pattern (using the preposition *to* after *go*).

   **go + noun**: *go home*: In this phrase, *to* is dropped. Students should memorize this as a "special case."

**ADDITIONAL VOCABULARY** Ask students if they can think of any other activities they do every day (such as *brush (your) teeth, exercise, check Facebook/Instagram, eat breakfast*) and put them on the board. (Note that talking about food and eating will be covered in Unit 12.) Students will be able to use this language later in the lesson.

**B** Cover **A**. Complete the sentences. Use the words in the box.

- Have students cover the words and pictures on page 68, and work on their own to complete the six sentences. Point out that they will use some of the verbs in the box more than once. Check answers as a class.

**SUPPORT** Allow students to refer to page 68 to complete the sentences.

**Answers**
1. get   2. take, get   3. go, start   4. finish   5. go, do
6. go

**C** 🔄 Say the sentences in **B** with a partner.

- Have students take turns saying the sentences in **B** with a partner.

**D** 🎯 Work in a small group. Play the game.

- Have students work in groups of three or four to play this game of Charades.

- Each group should begin by writing each of the nine actions on page 68 on a small slip of paper, shuffling the papers, and placing them face down in a pile.

- Give students a minute to review the new vocabulary. Then tell them to close their books.

- One student should be Student A (the "actor") while the other students are players. Student A should take the first paper and do the action. The players should try to guess the action as in the illustration. The first to call it out correctly gets the point.

- Variation: Instead of having students call out the answer, Student A should do the action, and each player should write his or her answer on a piece of paper. Then players should hold up their papers at the same time. Each correct answer gets a point.

- Student A should repeat the above step with all other words. At the end, the player with the most points is the winner.

- Play several rounds so that each group member gets a chance to be Student A.

**EXPANSION** Have students do the following exercise with a partner or small group.

**PREP WORK** Enlarge and print the grid below. Then bring one for every pair in class and tell students to cut it up so that they have 18 items total.

| get | up |
| take | a shower |
| get | dressed |
| go to | school |
| start | school |
| finish | school |
| go | home |
| do | homework |
| go to | bed |

Another option: Project the grid on the classroom wall and tell students (in pairs or small groups) to write each item (e.g., *get* or *a shower*) on a small slip of paper.

- Tell students to shuffle the papers and then place all of them face down on the desk in six rows with three cards in each row.

- To start the game, one student begins by turning over two papers. The goal is to find a matching pair that forms one of the new vocabulary phrases (e.g., *get + dressed, go to + school*.). If the papers do not form a matching pair, the player should turn over the papers (so they are face down again) and it's another player's turn.

- If the two papers form one of the new vocabulary phrases (e.g., *go to + school*), the player should say the phrase aloud and then try

to make a logical sentence (e.g., *I go to school at 7:30.*). If the student can do this, he/she takes that pair of papers and keeps them. If the student can't do this, he should turn over the papers (so they are face down again). Then it's another player's turn.

- Students should keep playing until they have picked up all of the word pairs. The player with the most pairs wins.

**E** Write sentences about your daily routine. Use the words from **A**.

- Tell students they're going to be writing three sentences about their daily routine. What's a typical day like for them? What things do they do? Tell students to focus on days that they go to school or work in their sentences, and to use the new vocabulary. (Note: Days of the week will be introduced in the speaking lesson.)

**F** Tell a partner about your day. Use your sentences in **E**.

- Have students tell a partner their sentences. Ask students: *Are your days similar or different?*

**G** Tell a new partner about your day. This time, don't read your sentences.

- Before students do this exercise, give them a couple of minutes to rehearse describing their day without reading their sentences. Then have students pair up with a new partner. This time, students should close their books and describe their daily routine. If they struggle, let them look back at their notes, but encourage them to try to talk as much as they can without reading.

**CHALLENGE / EXPANSION** Time students as they do the activity.

Round 1: Assign each pair of students the roles of Student A and Student B. Student As will all go first and will have 60 seconds to tell their partner about their daily routine, without reading their notes. (You may need to adjust this time depending on how much or little students have written.) At the end of 60 seconds, call out "Stop!" Students must stop talking, even if they're not finished. Then it's Student B's turn to talk for 60 seconds.

Rounds 2 & 3: In Round 2, have students pair up with a new partner. This time, give each student 45 seconds to explain his or her day. In Round 3, give them 30 seconds each to explain their day.

At the end of Round 3, take a class survey. As you say *Round 1,* have students raise their hands if they thought it was hard or easy to do. Do the same for Rounds 2 and 3. In this way, you can see if the activity got any easier for students as they repeated it. Research has shown that having students do this kind of exercise can help to improve accuracy and build spoken fluency.

# 2 GRAMMAR

This Grammar lesson will introduce five adverbs of frequency (*always, usually, often, sometimes,* and *never*) and focus on their meaning and position in a sentence.

**A** Look at the words. Say them with your teacher.

- Before presenting the language in the grammar box, which deals with the placement and usage of adverbs of frequency in the sentence, students must first have an understanding of what the different adverbs mean. Have students look at the chart. Note that this "frequency chart" is a rough approximation of meaning. These words don't correspond to any kind of exact percentages, however, by using a word like *usually* rather than *sometimes,* we are stating that an action occurs more frequently. If appropriate, give translations for these words in the students' native language.

- Go over the adverbs in the left column by reading them aloud and having students repeat. Ask them to tap out the syllables (including the stressed syllable) for each word. Ask them where the heaviest stress falls in each one (Answer: the first syllable). Note that the /t/ sound is silent in the word *often,* so it sounds more like "OFFen" when said aloud.

**B** 🔁 Complete the sentence. Use a word from **A**. Tell a partner.

- To give students some practice with meaning, have your students read the sentence and work silently. They should complete the sentence to make a statement that is true for themselves. Then ask students to get into pairs and share their answers.

- Finally, take a class poll. Have students raise their hands when they hear their sentence read

aloud (e.g., *I always get up around seven in the morning. I usually get up around seven in the morning.*).

**C** Study the chart.

- As a first step, go over the meanings of *early* and *late* by giving two examples: *I often get up at noon. I get up late. / I always get up at six in the morning. I get up early.*

**LANGUAGE NOTE** In this lesson, students are learning five common adverbs of frequency: *always, usually, often, sometimes,* and *never.* There are other words in this group, such as *normally, generally, frequently, occasionally, seldom, hardly ever,* and *rarely.* The number of adverbs presented here is limited so that students are not overwhelmed. Also, the five selected all have distinguishable different meanings, as opposed to teaching *hardly ever* and *rarely* together, which are pretty much identical in meaning. If appropriate, introduce *hardly ever* at this point, it falls between *sometimes* and *never* in the chart. Note that although *never* has a negative meaning, it is always paired with an affirmative verb, so we say *I'm never late* and not *I'm not never late.*

- Go over the sentences in the grammar chart, pointing out that the position of these adverbs in the sentences shifts according to whether they're used with the verb *be* or other verbs.

- Recycling the language that students have learned up to this point, say some sentences aloud and ask students to raise their hands for each one that is true for them. Some possible examples:

  *I always take a shower in the morning.*
  *I'm usually at school early.*
  *I sometimes study in a café.*
  *I often go home late.*
  *English class is sometimes fun.*
  *I never go shopping with my family.*
  *I usually have a lot of free time.*

**EXPANSION** Write the above sentences on the board. When students raise their hands to say the sentence is true for them, tell them to keep their hands raised for a moment. Then call on one of the students who didn't raise his or her hand. Ask that student to revise the sentence by changing the adverb to make it true for him/her. (For example, a student might say *I never take a shower in the morning. I take a bath in the evening.*)

**D** Read the sentences. Write new sentences. Use the blue words.

- Teach the meaning of the word *miss* (which in this case collocates with *class*, so it means "to be absent from class"). Read through the sentences together as a class. Then go over the first item together so students understand that they are to rewrite the sentences and insert the adverb of frequency into the correct spot in the sentence in each case.

- Go over the answers as a class. Ask several students to come to the front and write their answer for the second item on the board. (*I'm usually happy.*) Then look at each answer and ask the class *Is this one OK?* Do this for all of the items in the exercise.

**Answers**
1. I always do homework after school.   2. I'm usually happy.   3. I sometimes watch movies in the evening.
4. I'm often early to school.   5. I never miss class.
6. I often raise my hand in class.

**E** 🔄 Say the sentences in **D**. Are the sentences true for you? Tell your partner.

- Read the example with a student, then model with a different student using sentence 2.

- Put students into pairs and have them tell their partner which sentences are true for themselves.

**EXPANSION** Teach students some additional vocabulary by demonstrating how to ask a question with *why* and answer with *because*. Then, concentrating on items 1, 3, 4, and 6, have students practice asking *why*. Exchanges could go something like this:

*I always do homework after school. / Why? /
Because I have free time after school.
I sometimes watch movies in the evening. / Why? /
Because it's relaxing OR Because I like movies.
I'm often at school early. / Why? / Because I
get up early.
I often raise my hand in class. / Why? / Because I
like this class.*

**F** Put the words in order. Write the sentences.

- In this exercise, students are going to unscramble sentences that use adverbs of frequency. As a first step, go over the information in the Notice! box.

**LANGUAGE NOTE** Some of these adverbs can be placed in different positions in the sentence.

The important thing is that students are able to understand the rules in the grammar chart in **C** and produce correct sentences.

There are other rules about the position of adverbs, but it is important to keep things simple for students at this stage. The check marks that are followed by an asterisk in the chart below are the ones introduced in this lesson.

|  | always | often | usually | sometimes | never | Examples |
|---|---|---|---|---|---|---|
| after the verb *be* | ✓* | ✓* | ✓* | ✓* | ✓* | *I am always early.* |
| before other verbs | ✓* | ✓* | ✓* | ✓* | ✓* | *I never skip meals.* |
| initial position |  | ✓ | ✓ | ✓* |  | *Usually I get up at 7:00.* |
| end position |  |  |  | ✓* |  | *I get up late sometimes.* |

- Give students time to unscramble the sentences. You may want to have them pair up with a partner and go over their answers (checking for word order, punctuation, spelling, and capitalization) before reviewing the answers as a class.

**CHALLENGE** Another way to do this exercise is to have students keep their books closed. Write the six items on the board and leave a blank space where the verb goes. So the first two items would look like this:

1. ---- / books / she / comic / never
2. math / always / ---- / interesting / class

Students have to unscramble the sentences in the same way, but they also have to choose a suitable verb (for item 1, for example, you could go with *read* or *buy*) as well as the correct form of the verb (*reads* or *buys*). For the second item, students would have to choose the correct form of the verb *be* (which would be *is*).

**Answers**
1. She never reads comic books.   2. Math class is always interesting.   3. Sometimes I have an appointment after school. OR I sometimes have an appointment after school. OR I have an appointment after school sometimes.   4. My teacher is never sad.   5. They usually study in a café.   6. English tests are often difficult.

**G** 🔄 Complete the sentences. Practice them with a partner.

- The next three exercises focus on the theme of the first day of school. In this exercise, students are going to familiarize themselves with the language that they will need to use throughout.

- Introduce the two new vocabulary items (*choose* and *nervous*). For the first one, place two pens on a desk in front of you. As you pick one up, say *I choose this one.* To define the word *nervous,* you can tell students about a situation (e.g, right before the start of a big test) that makes you nervous.

- The top row in the chart represents four things that a person might do (or how they might feel) the night before in preparation for the first day of school: choosing (or setting out) the outfit that you're going to wear the next day, getting your backpack ready with things you need for the day, going to bed early in order to get a good night's sleep, and feeling a little nervous. The bottom row lists four things that might occur or be felt in the morning: sleeping through one's alarm (sleeping late), taking a shower to get ready, going to school early, and feeling excited.

- Make sure students understand the vocabulary. To check, you can have them cover up the words with a piece of paper and try to recall the sentence that goes with each picture (e.g., *I choose my clothes.*).

- Note that students have learned the word *exciting* in a previous unit. In item 8 they will see the word *excited.* You can explain to them that *the first day of school is exciting* while *I feel excited about the first day of school.*

**CLASSROOM MANAGEMENT** This exercise could also work as "My first day of work" (if you are teaching older students).

**H** 🔊 **Track 57** Listen. Write the missing words in **G**.

- Students are now familiar with the vocabulary. Play the audio and have them fill in the missing adverbs of frequency. Go over the answers as a class.

**Answers**
1. often  2. usually  3. Sometimes  4. never
5. sometimes  6. always  7. usually  8. always

**I** 🔄 Think about the first day of school for you. What do you do? Tell a partner. Use adverbs.

- Using the sentences in **G** as a model, have students take a moment and think about how they would complete the different tasks before their own first day of school. Read the example with a student.

- Have students get into pairs and take turns telling their partner about what they do and how they feel. They should go sentence by sentence and keep track of any items where they both wrote the same answer.

- Come together as a class and, starting with number 8, count down to 0. As you read each number, ask the pairs to raise their hands if they and their partner matched on that number of items. For example, if two students matched answers on items 2 and 6 (*I usually check my backpack* and *I always take a shower*), then they would raise their hands when you say the number "2." In this way, you'll see which pairs of students have similar habits to each other. Which pair(s) matched the most number of items?

**PRONUNCIATION TIP**

The sound /I/ is a significant problem for students from different language backgrounds and requires a lot of awareness raising and practice. Have students go back to pages 68, 69, and 70 to look for words that have the letter i pronounced /I/: *fin̲ish, mill̲ions, i̲n, swi̲m, practi̲ce, i̲s, vi̲deo, wi̲th, mi̲x, morn̲ing, eveni̲ng, thi̲s, mi̲ss, uni̲t.*

# 3 SPEAKING

In this Speaking lesson, students will practice talking about their weekends.

**A** Look at the photo. Say the days of the week with your teacher. Then answer the questions.

- Do the following with the class:

- Look at the photo on the top of the page and say the days of the week with students.

**EXPANSION** Write the days of the week on the board out of order and erase three of them. Have a volunteer come to the front of the class; then ask students which days are missing. Have the volunteer write the missing days as the class calls them out. Repeat this several times with different student volunteers.

- Then ask questions 1 and 2 and take answers from the class.

- Introduce the word *weekend.* Then ask question 3.

**CULTURE NOTE** The weekend is the day or two when many people have time off from work or school. Weekend days around the world vary. In some countries, people have Saturday and Sunday off. In other countries, people work or go to school all or half a day on Saturday and then have Sunday off. In a number of countries in the Middle East, the weekend is typically Friday and Saturday.

**ADDITIONAL VOCABULARY** To wish someone a good weekend (as a way of saying *goodbye*), you can say *Have a good/nice weekend!* The reply to this is *You too.*

**B** Say the sentences in the Useful Language box with your teacher.

- Say the question about the weekend in the Useful Language box with students. Point out that the question asks about things a person *usually* does on weekends; it is not asking about plans for the upcoming weekend.

- Then introduce the replies to the question, and say them with the class.

  *Not much.* means *I don't do a lot.* (This person has a lot of free time on the weekend.)

  *I'm really busy.* means *I do a lot of things.* (Note that the word *really* = *very*, and *busy* = *very active, doing a lot.*)

**C** 🔊 Track 58 Read and listen to the conversation.

- Have students read the dialogue to themselves silently. Then play the audio once through.

- For additional practice, play the audio again.

**LANGUAGE NOTE** ON + DAY OF THE WEEK
After students listen to the dialogue, direct their attention to the Notice! note. The preposition *on* is used to specify days or dates. (This lesson focuses on using *on* with <u>days</u> of the week and the weekend. Students will learn how to use *on* with <u>dates</u> in Unit 11.)

Look at the example sentences in the Notice! note. Point out that students can be more specific about their routines by adding a word like *morning, afternoon,* or *evening/night* after the day of the week: *I work on Saturday morning. On Sunday night, I do homework.*

Note, too, that *on* is also used with *the weekend*: *What do you usually do <u>on the weekend</u>?*

**LANGUAGE NOTE** Note the meaning of this language in the dialogue for students as needed:

*What about you?* asks for an answer or opinion about something said (e.g., *I like that TV show. What about you?* or *I don't do much on the weekend. What about you?*)

*Wow* is a word used to show surprise.

**D** 🔄 Answer the questions with a partner.

- Have students answer the questions about the dialogue in **C**.

**Answers**
1. Bill usually gets up late. Sometimes, he sees his friends. Nadia has class on Saturday morning. Then she works on Saturday afternoon. On Sunday, she does homework.
2. On the weekend, Nadia is busy. Bill has a lot of free time.

**E** 🔄 Say the conversation in **C** with your partner.

- Have students work in pairs to practice the conversation in **C**. After they've done it once, have them change roles and practice again.

**F** What do you do on the weekend? Check (✓) the activities.

- Before students answer the question, go over the activities with them. Then have students work on their own to do the exercise. They can also add their own ideas.

**LANGUAGE NOTE** ACTIVITIES WITH *GO*
Draw students' attention to the Notice! note about activities with *go;* point out the patterns.

1. **go to + a/the + noun**: *go to a soccer game, go to the beach, go to the movies*

*Go* is often followed by the preposition *to* in order to show movement from one place to another. It's best not to get into details about the usage of *a/ an* vs. *the* here. Students can simply memorize the different expressions.

2. **go to + noun**: *go to school, go to bed, go to work*

For some nouns (*school, work, bed*), we drop *a/ an* or *the*, but still use *to.* Students learned this language in the Vocabulary lesson.

3. **go + ing word**: *go shopping, go swimming*

This pattern is often used to describe activities we do in our free time. Note that *to* is not used.

**ADDITIONAL VOCABULARY** Other weekend activities that students may want to talk about include: *clean, cook, play soccer, relax /sleep, work*

**G** ⟳ Work with a partner. Say the conversation in **C** again. Use your own information and the ideas in **F**.

- Have students say the dialogue in **C** again using the expressions in the Useful Language box and their ideas in **F**.

**CHALLENGE** Have students say the dialogue again. This time, though, tell them to keep the conversation going by inviting their partner to do something on the weekend using an idea from **F** and *Are you free (this weekend)?* and *Let's…* (which were both introduced in Unit 9).

**H** ⬡ Ask three classmates about their weekends. Complete the chart.

- Have students interview different classmates about their weekends and take notes in the chart.

**I** ⟳ Tell a new partner your answers in **H**. Are the people busy on the weekend or not?

- Point out the example, then model the activity with a student using information about one of the students in the class. Ask him or her, *Is (name) busy on the weekend?* Have students pair up and explain their answers to a new partner.

**J** ⟳ What are popular weekend activities in your class? Tell your partner.

- With their partner, have students identify which weekend activities were mentioned most often. Have pairs join to make groups of four and compare which activities are the most popular. Then have each group share their answers with the class.

# 11 IMPORTANT DAYS

## 1 VOCABULARY

In this Vocabulary lesson, students will learn to say months and dates, and talk about birthdays.

**A** 🔊 **Track 59** Listen and say the months of the year.

- Before students listen to the audio, do the following:

  Read the unit title aloud. Then ask students if they can name any important days or holidays, provide examples as necessary, and write all of their ideas on the board. You'll use these later in the lesson.

- Introduce the word *month,* and ask students if they can say any in English without looking in the book.

- Have students look at the twelve months and read the words to themselves silently.

- Then play the audio. As the speaker says a month, students should repeat it.

**B** 🔁 Work with a partner. Say the months. Then change roles and repeat.

**STUDENT A:** Close your book. Say the months.
**STUDENT B:** Check Student A's answers.

- Give students a minute or so to review the months by themselves. Then have students work in pairs. Student A should close his or her book and say the months aloud, and Student B should check A's answers. Then students should change roles.

**SUPPORT** Allow students to refer to their books the first time they say the months aloud to a partner. The second time, they should close their books.

**EXPANSION** 1. Have students take turns saying the months rapidly back and forth in pairs (e.g., A says *January,* B says *February,* A says *March,* B says *April,* and so on). 2. Have students stand in

a circle of 4–5 people. (Depending on the size of your class, you may have multiple circles.) Have students go around the circle with each person saying a month in the correct order (e.g., Student A says *January,* B says *February,* C says *March,* D says *April,* and so on). If a person hesitates or forgets the next month (e.g., if Student E says *March* instead of *May*), that student is out. Keep playing until only one student is left standing. To make the exercise more challenging, have students periodically say the months in reverse order (*December, November, October...*).

**C** Choose a month. Complete the sentence.

- Have students work on their own to choose a month and complete the sentence. For example, *This month starts with the letter O* (Answer: *October*).

**D** 🔁 Cover the months in **A**. Say your sentence in **C**. Your partner says the month.

- Have students work in pairs say their sentences for a partner to guess. If a student says a letter for which there is more than one month (e.g., M: *May, March*), the other student can keep guessing until he/she gets the correct month. Have students repeat the exercise with different partners.

**EXPANSION** Put students in small groups. One student begins by saying his or her sentence (*This month starts with the letter A*). The others write their answers on pieces of paper (which is good for spelling practice) and hold up their papers at the same time. Each correct answer gets a point. Have students repeat the exercise several times.

**E** 🔊 **Track 60** Listen and repeat.

- Before students listen to the audio, do the following:

  Write the numbers *one, two, three, four* on the board. Next to each, write its corresponding ordinal number: *first, second, third, fourth.*

- Remind students that they already know numbers like *one, two, three, four*, etc. Now they are going to learn related words (*first, second, third, fourth*, etc.) used for listing things in order.

- Then play the audio. As the speaker says a number, students should repeat it. After students say the new vocabulary, help them notice the points mentioned in the language note below.

**LANGUAGE NOTE** ORDINAL NUMBERS
In most cases, ordinal numbers are formed by adding *th* to the regular number (e.g., *four – fourth, six – sixth, eleven – eleventh*).

Important exceptions to the rule above include the first three numbers (*first, second, third*). Also, in *five* and *twelve*, the *v* changes to an *f* (*five – fifth, twelve – twelfth*) and the letter *e* is dropped. (Note, too, the vowel shift from *five* and *fifth*.) The *e* is also dropped when you go from *nine* to *ninth*.

PRONUNCIATION TIP
Practice saying some of the numbers that end in *th* with students, helping them notice how the final sound is pronounced (*fourth*). Some learners will have a tendency to pronounce the final sound as *t* (as in *fort*) or *s* (as in *force*), or to drop it altogether.

- Draw students' attention to the spelling change that happens for the number 20 (*twenty – twentieth*), and the pattern for counting from 21 to 29: *twenty-first, twenty-second, twenty-third, twenty-fourth*, and so on. When these numbers are written out, a hyphen is used.

- Note that once students have learned how to spell the numbers 20th–29th, they will know the spelling and pronunciation rules they need to be able to count up to 100.

**ADDITIONAL VOCABULARY** *40th—fortieth, 50th—fiftieth, 60th—sixtieth, 70th—seventieth, 80th—eightieth, 90th—ninetieth, 100th—one hundredth*

Informally, ordinal numbers can be written as follows: the numeral + the last two letters of the word (e.g., *first = 1st, fourth = 4th*).

**EXPANSION** 1. Put these numbers on the board and have students take turns saying them with a partner.

| 1st | 2nd | 5th | 6th | 12th | 13th |
|-----|-----|-----|-----|------|------|
| 20th | 21st | 23rd | 24th | 30th | 31st |

In round 1, students can refer to their books for support; in round two, they should cover the word list in **E** and say them again. For more practice, have students write their own numbers (they can go beyond 30th) and quiz their partner. 2. Put students in pairs. Write this sentence on the board: *What is the ___ month of the year?* Then write an ordinal number in the blank space on the board (e.g., *3rd*). Student A must now ask Student B the question: *What is the third month of the year?* Student B should answer *March*. Then erase that number and write a new one. Now it's Student B's turn to ask the question. Keep doing this until you've covered all twelve months. For more practice, have a student volunteer write the numbers on the board. This exercise can also be done in small groups. 3. Have students create flashcards for the numbers. On each card (or slip of paper), they should write a number on the front (e.g., 1st) and the corresponding word on the back (e.g., first). Have students mix up their cards and then quiz each other.

PRONUNCIATION TIP
Help students see that the voiceless /θ/ sound (as in fourth /fɔrθ/) is made by placing the tongue between the upper and lower front teeth. Demonstrate this articulation for them and have them imitate you. Next, use the ordinal numbers to practice them. Then, have students make a line, and elicit the order they are in.

**F** 🔊 Track 61 Listen. Write the dates.

- Before students listen, write on the board: *What is the date today?* Take ideas from the class.

- Then draw students' attention to the Notice! about saying and writing the date.

**LANGUAGE NOTE** DATE VERSUS DAY
Make sure that students understand the difference between the words *date* and *day*. An example of the date is April 3, 2017. The word *day* usually refers to a day of the week (e.g., *Monday*). It can also refer to a specific calendar day (e.g., Today is the third.).

**SAYING AND WRITING THE DATE IN THE U.S.**

1. In the US, the date is said and written in this order: month / day / year (*July 4, 2017*)

2. People say the date like this: *It's July fourth.*

3. People write the date like this: *It's July 4.*

4. Months are often abbreviated to three or four letters as follows (*May, June, July* are not shortened): *Jan, Feb, Mar, Apr, May, June, July, Aug, Sept, Oct, Nov, Dec.*

5. People also use numbers to write the date (e.g., *7/4*). The month (*7*) is first and the day (*4*) second.

• Finally, tell students they are going to listen as a person says twelve different dates. Do the first one (*July 4*) as an example. When students write their answers, they can write out the entire month (if it's short), use an abbreviation (*Oct 1*), or use numbers (*12/23*).

**Answers**
1. July 4   2. March 2   3. May 1   4. October 11
5. September 3   6. August 25   7. January 31
8. April 13   9. February 22   10. November 16
11. June 30   12. December 10

**G** Say the dates in **F** with a partner. Take turns.

• Have students check their answers in **F** with a partner by taking turns and saying the dates.

**H** Complete the sentence. Write the month and day.

• Introduce the word *birthday* and make sure students understand the meaning. Then have students complete the sentence with their birthday date, writing the month and day only (e.g., *October 5*).

• Draw students' attention to the Notice! note on using *in* and *on* with dates.

**LANGUAGE NOTE** USING *IN* WITH MONTHS AND *ON* WITH DATES

*in* + month: My birthday is in May.

*on* + date:  My birthday is on May 22.

For practice with *in* and *on,* have students look back at the "important days" you wrote on the board before the class did **A**. Ask them to say the date of each important day using *in* and *on* (e.g., *Christmas is in December. It's on December 25.*)

**I** Write four different months in the chart.

• In the first column, students should write four different months to complete the question (e.g., *Is your birthday in July?*).

**J** Play the game with your class.

• Have students circulate asking the question in the chart using the months they've written (e.g., *Is your birthday in July?*). When another student answers *yes,* that student should say when exactly his or her birthday is, as in the model dialogue on the page (*Yes, it's on July 1.*). The goal is to be the first student to complete the chart. That student can either call out "Stop!" or sit down.

**EXPANSION** 1. Have the student who completed his or her chart first say the answers aloud for the class. Put this sentence on the board to help the student: _____'s birthday is _____. (e.g., *Alec's birthday is on July 1.*) 2. For additional practice, have students repeat the game with four different months. 3. Does anyone in class have a birthday coming up soon? If so, how old is he/she? Teach the class what to say to a person on his or her birthday: *Happy (21st) birthday!* 4. Ask students this question: In your country, what birthdays are important (1st, 13th, 15th, 20th, 21st, 60th)? Have students work on their own or in pairs to create a simple collage that highlights an important birthday and shows photos of things that happen. Help with vocabulary as needed. Students can then share these in small groups.

# 2 GRAMMAR

This Grammar lesson will introduce *Wh-* questions with verbs other than *be* and contrast them with *Yes / No* questions (which students have already learned).

**A** Study the chart.

**LANGUAGE NOTE** This unit will introduce *Wh-* question words that are used to ask about:

information or things (*What*)
place or position (*Where*)
a person's identity (*Who*)

date and time (*When*) and
the way to do something (*How*)

Students may not be familiar with questions with *How,* so you can write an example on the board: *How do you spell your name?* This unit does not touch on *wh-* question words used to ask about: reasons (*Why*), possession (*Whose*), and information about specific things (*Which*) to make it more manageable for students.

- Students learned *Yes / No* questions with verbs other than *be* in *Put it Together 3.* To do a quick review of those questions and the short answers that follow (with books closed), ask different students questions like these:

  *Do you have a big family? Do you like hip hop? Does she speak English? Does class start soon? Do they have homework? Do they work in an office?*

- After they have answered a few *Yes / No* questions correctly, write this question on the board: *Does class start soon?* Introduce the question word *when* and explain how it is used. Then write the word *When* in front of the sentence on the board, and cross out the word *soon* at the end of the sentence. (You should now see the question *When does class start?* on the board.) Students should then answer the question. In this way you can show students that *Wh-* questions are quite easy to form once you have the correct word order — you just place the question word at the front.

- Ask students to open their books to page 76. Go through all the questions and answers in the chart with the students. Then focus on only the *Wh-* questions. Ask three or four different students the same question from the chart. Each student should give a different answer (without looking at their books). For example, for the question *Where do you live?* Students could answer with their city, state, country, or neighborhood. *What do they study?* Students could give the name of any school subject, such as *history* or *art.* *How does she go to school?* Students can answer with *by car, by train, by subway,* etc. (If it comes up naturally here, you can also teach the expression *on foot.*)

### PRONUNCIATION TIP

In questions, *do* and *does* are often pronounced /də/ and /dəz/ when they have no stress.

**CHALLENGE** Write the words *long* and *short* on the board. As you ask each question point to one of the words, students then have to answer your question with the "long answer" or the "short answer."

**B** Match the questions and answers.

- In this exercise, students should match the *Wh-* questions on the left with their answers on the right. (Note that some of the responses are "long answers," whereas others are "short answers." Since you have just practiced them in the previous exercise, it should be familiar to your students.) Ask students to read through all of the questions on the left and make sure they understand the meaning. They may not know the word *presents* (gifts). Point out the Notice! note and the meaning of the question: *What do you do?*

- Give students time to do the exercise and check their answers with a partner. Then go over the answers together as a class.

**CHALLENGE** Students should close their books as you will be turning this into a listening exercise.

**PREP WORK** Write the responses to the questions (items a-h in the right hand column) on the board ahead of time. Tell each student (or team of students) that they will have five seconds to choose the correct answer to your question from the list on the board. Go to the first student and read the first question (*Where do you live?*) If the student chooses *c,* then that's correct and you erase the answer from the board. If the time runs out because the student can't answer fast enough, go to the next student and ask a *different* question and see if that student can come up with the answer in five seconds. As each question gets answered and the list of responses gets smaller, the activity should become easier. Keep going until all of the questions have been answered.

**Answers**
1. c   2. g   3. e   4. a   5. d   6. h   7. b   8. f

**C** 🔁 Work with a partner. Ask and answer the questions in **B**.

- Have students get into pairs and ask and answer the questions with a partner. They should give answers that are true for their real-life situations.

- Students can rotate for one or two rounds, asking the questions to different partners. At the end of the last round, call on different pairs to ask and answer one of the questions from the list. They can do this by reading the question in their books and then looking up to say the question.

**CHALLENGE** For this last part, to stop students from just reading the questions directly from their books, have them look at the question and then tell them to wait for 5–7 seconds before asking it to their partner (to see if they can remember it).

**D** 🔊 Track 62 Dai is checking in to his new class. Complete the questions. Then listen and check your answers.

- In this exercise, students are going to read and listen to a conversation that takes place at school as Dai (a student) reports for his first day of classes. Point out that *check in* (in the Word Bank) means to arrive and register at a place. Ask students where they might use the word *check in* (possible answers: at a hotel, airport, or school).

- Ask students to open their books to page 76 and give them one minute to skim the first few lines of the dialogue. Then ask them to close their books.

- Tell students that it's OK if they don't know the answers perfectly. Then ask them a couple of comprehension questions like this:

  *Who is Dai?* (He's a student.)
  *Where is he?* (He's at school.)
  *What day is it?* (It's the first day of school.)

- Another option would be to give True-False statements to test comprehension:

  *Dai is a student.* (True)
  *He's at home.* (False)
  *His class is tomorrow.* (False)

- Once students understand the context for the conversation (Dai reporting to school), have them read through the dialogue and predict the answers. (Make certain students know the meaning of the word *hall* and the usage of *get* (as in "arrive") in the conversation.) Then play the audio and have them check their answers.

**Answers**

Dai: Good morning. I'm Dai. Dai Suzuki.
Woman: Good morning, Dai. Hmm… OK, I see your name. You're checked in.
Dai: Thanks. <u>Where</u> does the class <u>meet</u>?
Woman: You're in Room 11.
Dai: OK. How <u>do</u> I <u>get</u> there?
Woman: Go straight down the hall and turn right. It's the second door on your left.
Dai: Great. <u>When</u> <u>does</u> the class start?
Woman: Let's see… in about ten minutes.
Dai: Oh, and <u>what time</u> does it <u>finish</u>?
Woman: At 9:15.
Dai: Thanks a lot.

**E** 🔄 Say the conversation in **D** with a partner. Use your own names and your own answers.

- Students should now use the conversation in **D** as a model and work with a partner to come up with their own version. Once each pair has their own conversation, have them practice it. Students should take turns playing the roles of the students and the school employee.

- Ask some students to perform their conversations for the class. (Since it's a long conversation, they can refer to their papers, but encourage them to read and look up, not to just bury their faces in their papers.)

**SUPPORT** To help students in preparing to create their own versions, go through the conversation in **D** and highlight the words that students will need to replace with their own information.

**F** 🔄 Work with a partner. Look up these words in your dictionary.

- Students will need to know the words in the Word Bank in order to complete the remaining exercises in the lesson.

**CLASSROOM MANAGEMENT** To speed up this process, put students into groups of four and have each student in the group look up one of the words in their dictionary. Then ask each student to tell their group about their word. Finally, go over the words as a class and answer any questions that students may have.

**G** Think about New Year's Eve. Complete the YES and NO questions. Write the missing words.

- In this exercise, students are going to create some questions about New Year's Eve. First, point out the information in the Notice! box.

**CULTURE NOTE** In some places, people follow a lunar calendar and celebrate New Year's at different times. (The Chinese New Year, for example, traditionally begins at the end of January or the beginning of February and lasts for a month.) In the Jewish and Muslim faiths, the New Year is celebrated in the fall. Most festivities, however, begin on December 31st and extend into January 1st, or New Year's Day. During this time people do things like go to parties, eat special foods, and watch fireworks. In this activity, students are going to talk about their own experience of New Year's festivities and traditions.

- First have your students look at the questions. They should fill in the missing *Wh-* word for each one. Go over the answers as a class.

**Answers**
**YES** box: What, When, Who, What
**NO** box: What, Where, What, What

**H** Think about the first question in **G**. Choose the YES or NO box and answer the questions.

- Now that students have completed the questions in **G**, they should work individually and go back to answer the question at the top of chart: *Do you have a party on New Year's Eve?* If they or their friends and family have a party, then their answer is YES and they should answer the four questions in the YES box. If their answer to the question is NO, then they should answer the questions in the NO box.

**CLASSROOM MANAGEMENT** Students don't need to write out their answers to these questions unless you have the time and want them to do so. Just get them to think about their answers. Circulate around the room, assisting students with vocabulary as necessary. The important thing is that each student has the answers (in some form) to four of the questions in **G**.

- Students' answers will vary depending on their own experiences, but here are some possible answers to the questions:

| | |
|---|---|
| *What do you buy for the party?* | (noisemakers, cake, drinks, balloons) |
| *When do you start the party?* | (after dinner, at 10 p.m., just before midnight) |
| *Who do you invite?* | (family and friends) |
| *What do you serve?* | (a round cake with gold or silver coins baked inside (Greece), champagne and caviar (Russia), grapes (midnight in Spain), rice cake soup (Korea)) |
| *What do you do?* | (hang out with friends) |
| *Where do you go?* | (a party, a temple, a church) |
| *What do you wear?* | (nothing special, a lucky necklace) |
| *What do you say?* | (Happy New Year! Best Wishes for 2019 / the New Year!) |

**I** Ask a partner the questions in **G**. Take turns. Are your plans similar or different?

- Put students into pairs. To show them how the activity will work, go over the model conversation on the page. When the word *noisemaker* comes up in the conversation, point to it in the picture on the right.

- Students should now ask their partners the appropriate questions.

- Come back together as a class. As you read each question, ask individual students to tell you about their partner's answer. For example, when you say the question *When does your partner start his/her party?* a student might tell the class: *My partner is Gregor. His party starts at 10 p.m. on New Year's Eve. The party ends at 10 a.m. the next day!*

# 3 SPEAKING

In this Speaking lesson, students will practice saying how certain or uncertain they are about something.

**A** Look at the picture. Answer the questions.

- Look at the photo on the page and tell students to read the caption. (You can use the photo to illustrate the meaning of the word *costume*.) Ask: *What special day is it? What country?* Elicit anything students already know about Halloween, ask, *When is Halloween?* Do students know the month? The exact day? (October 31st) If not, encourage students to use their phones and find out.

- Then ask the question on the page:
1. What do people do on Halloween?

**CULTURE NOTE** Halloween is celebrated on Oct. 31st. In the U.S., children dress up like ghosts, witches, superheroes, and other characters. They go door to door, asking for candy by saying "Trick or treat!" ("Give me a treat or I will play a trick on you!"). In recent years, more adults celebrate Halloween by dressing up and going to costume parties.

**B** Say the sentences in the Useful Language box with your teacher.

- Ask the question about the Halloween party in the Useful Language box. Then introduce the replies to the question and say them with the class.

- In the first reply (*It's this Saturday.*), the speaker is certain; he knows when the party is.

- In the second reply (*I'm not sure.*), the speaker is not certain, but he has an idea and so he asks the question: *Is it on Saturday?*

- In the third reply (*I don't know* or *I have no idea*), the speaker doesn't know the answer at all. The two expressions mean the same thing.

**C** 🔊 Track 63 Look at the calendar. Then read and listen to the conversation.

- Have students look at the activities listed on the calendar. One is the Halloween party; the other two are different festivals. Make sure students understand the meaning of the word *festival* and then ask them: *What happens at a film festival? At a food festival?*

- Then have students read the dialogue to themselves silently. Finally, play the audio once through. For additional practice, play the audio again.

**LANGUAGE NOTE** The days of the week are sometimes abbreviated (as they are in the schedule on page 78) as follows: *Mon, Tues, Wed, Thurs, Fri, Sat, Sun.*

**D** 🔄 Answer the questions with a partner.

- Have students answer the questions about the dialogue in **C**.

**Answers**
1. The Halloween party is on Saturday, October 30.
2. It starts at 9:00.

**E** 🔄 Work with a partner. Say the conversation in **C**.

- Have students work in pairs to practice the conversation in **C**. After they've done it once, have them change roles and practice again.

**F** 🔄 Work with a partner. Say the conversation in **C** again. Talk about the film festival. Use the information on the calendar and a different expression.

- Have students substitute information about the film festival in the dialogue and encourage them to use different language to express uncertainty (*I don't know*, or *I have no idea.*)

**G** 🔄 Change roles. This time, talk about the food festival.

- Have students change roles, and this time substitute information about the food festival in the dialogue. Encourage them to use different language to express uncertainty.

**H** Look at each important day. When is it? Write the date or check (✓) "Don't know."

- Before students write their answers, do the following:

  Review the meaning of the words in the Word Bank. You can illustrate the meaning of *last* by writing some example dates on the board showing the first and last day of school (e.g., January 3-April 10). Using the example, ask students: *When is the first day of school? When is the last day of school?* Then introduce the four seasons: spring, summer, fall, winter. You can translate these into students' native language, if appropriate, or have them look up the words in their dictionaries. Ask students which season is their favorite.

- Have students read the important days in the chart, and make sure they understand each one.

- Then have students complete the chart. Model what to do for them: if they know the date, they should write it; if they only know the month, they can just write that. If they don't know when the event happens, they should check "Don't know."

**I** 🔄 Work with a partner. Ask questions about the important days. Take turns.

- Put students in pairs and have them take turns asking questions about the days in the chart. Model what to do by having students read the model dialogue on the page. Students can use their phones to help them check their answers.

**Answers**
The last day of school: Answers will vary.
Mother's Day: Answers will vary.
Earth Day: April 22
The first day of winter: December 21 (Northern Hemisphere); June 21 (Southern Hemisphere)

**J** On your own, write four important days and their dates in your notebook.

- Have students work on their own to write four different important days and their dates in their notebooks. Students can list holidays, important days at school, the first or last day of a season, etc. Help with vocabulary as needed.

**K** 🔁 Work with a partner. Play the game. Take turns.

> **STUDENT A:** Ask a *When is…?* question about a day in **J**.
>
> **STUDENT B:** Guess the correct answer and get points.

- Put students in pairs. Model how the game is played, using the example dialogue on the page. Student A begins by asking about one of his/her important days (e.g., *When is Father's Day?*). Student B has to guess. If he guesses the month correctly, he gets one point. If he knows both the month and day, he gets two points.

- This game can also be played in teams, in which one pair comes up with the list of important days (and their dates). Another pair does the same. Then the pairs get together. Pair 1 asks their questions; Pair 2 tries to answer correctly and get as many points as they can. Then they change roles and repeat. The pair with the most points wins.

**EXPANSION** Research and assign each student a different special day. Ideally, the day will be celebrated in a different country or be an international event. It can be a holiday, festival, or special occasion (e.g., Carnival, Day of the Dead, Holi), or one that is more playful (e.g., Star Wars Day, White Day), or a day that raises awareness about a social issue (e.g., Earth Day, World AIDS Day).

- Project the questions below on the classroom wall and tell students to research and answer them in their notebooks.

1. *Where does <name of important day> happen?*
2. *When does it happen?*
3. *What do people usually do on this day?*
4. *Do people say anything special on this day? What do they say?*

- After students complete their research, put them in pairs and tell them to do the following:

> **STUDENT A:** Tell a partner the name of your important day. Ask your partner the four questions. Then tell your partner the answers as necessary.
>
> **STUDENT B:** Answer your partner's questions. If you don't know the answer, use an expression in the Useful Language box on page 78.

- Go over the example in the book by reading it with a student.

# 12 FOOD

## 1 VOCABULARY

In this Vocabulary lesson, students will learn to talk about different food and drinks in English.

**A** 🔊 **Track 64** Look at the pictures. Listen and repeat.

- Before students listen to the audio, do the following:

  Say the unit title (*Food*) aloud with the class. Also introduce the word *drink*. Make sure students understand both words.

**LANGUAGE NOTE** The word *drink* can be both a noun and a verb, and students will see both forms in this lesson: *Do you want a drink?* (noun) *I don't drink coffee.* (verb)

- Then ask students if they can name any food or drinks in English (without looking at their books). Write their ideas on the board.

- Have students look at the photos on page 80 and read the words to themselves silently.

- Then play the audio. As the speaker says a food or drink, students should point to it and repeat.

**NOTE** For photos with multiple items, it may be helpful to point to each thing in the photo (e.g., *cereal, fruit, juice*), so students know which is being said.

**ADDITIONAL VOCABULARY** After students listen, look again at the photos.

- Look at the photo with the tea. Point to the cubes and ask students if they know what this is in English (Answer: *sugar*).

- Look at the photo with the cereal, fruit, coffee, and orange juice. Write the word *fruit* on the board. Then point to the different pieces of fruit in the photo and see if students can name them

(*strawberry, banana*). Write these words under the word *fruit*. Ask students if they can name any other types of fruit in English (e.g., *apple, orange, pear*) and write them on the board.

- In the same photo, point to the orange juice. Note that this drink is often called *OJ* (pronounced as the letters O-J). Ask students if they can name any other types of juice (e.g., *apple juice, grape juice*) and write them on the board under drinks. Can the students add any other drinks in English?

- Look at the photo of the pizza. Ask students what is on the pizza (Answer: *tomatoes, olives, cheese*). Point out that there are also tomatoes in the bowl of pasta.

- Look at the background photo on the page, and see if students can identify any of the items being sold (e.g., *eggs, fish, pineapples, bananas*).

**CULTURE NOTE** 1. *Fries* (sometimes called *French fries*) are potato slices that have been fried (cooked in oil). They are often served with salt and ketchup and eaten as a snack or part of a larger meal. In the U.K., they're called *chips*. 2. The tea pictured is commonly served in Morocco and other North African countries. Traditionally, hot water is poured over green tea, mint and sugar are added, and the drink is served in glasses. 3. The woman in the background photo is selling food at the Siti Khadijah Central Market in Kota Bharu, a city in Malaysia. This large market is run primarily by women and sells everything from fresh fruit and vegetables, and meat and fish to prepared foods and desserts. It's an ideal place to sample the local cuisine.

**B** 🔊 **Track 65** Listen and repeat again. Notice *and*.

**PRONUNCIATION** Before students listen, direct their attention to the Notice! note. Explain that in spoken English, the word *and* is often shortened to just /n/ when joining two words (as in the example on the page). Then play the audio and have students listen and repeat.

**C** 🔁 Work with a partner. Cover the words under the photos. Say the food and drinks.

- Give students a minute or so to study the words on page 80. Then have students work in pairs. Tell them to take a piece of paper and cover the row of words below the top three photos so that they see only the pictures. Students should take turns saying the item(s) in each photo. As they say the food or drink, they should point to it in the photo.

- Students should do the same thing with the rest of the pictures, moving the paper down on the page as they complete a row of photos. For additional practice, have students repeat the exercise with a new partner.

**EXPANSION** Have students create flashcards in one of the two ways suggested below to practice the new vocabulary and quiz each other. Note: students can handwrite their cards or use an online flashcard-maker tool.

**Option 1:** On each card, students should write the word in English on the front (e.g., *rice*) and the corresponding word in their own native language on the back (e.g., *arroz*).

**Option 2:** Have students find photos or draw their own pictures of the different foods and drinks. On each card, they should put a photo or drawing on the front and the corresponding word(s) on the back (e.g., *chicken and rice*).

**D** 🔊 **Track 66** Say the words in the Word Bank. Then listen to the speaker. Number the photos (1–8) on page 80.

- Say the vocabulary in the Word Bank with the class and review each item's meaning.

- Start by introducing the verbs *eat* and *drink*. You can act out their meanings and put these sentences on the board as well: *I eat lunch at noon. I drink coffee in the morning.*

- Students already know *lunch* (from Unit 9). You can explain that you eat *breakfast* in the morning and *dinner* in the evening. *Dessert* is something sweet that people eat, usually at the end of lunch or dinner.

- Then have students look at the photos on page 80. Ask: *What do you eat and drink for breakfast? lunch? dinner? dessert?* Take ideas from the class.

**NOTICE** Students are learning a number of new vocabulary items in this lesson and the unit. Encourage them to organize this language in their notebooks to help them study and remember the new words. One way of categorizing the new vocabulary is under the headers *breakfast, lunch/dinner, dessert/snacks, drinks.* (Some items may be written in more than one category, of course.) Demonstrate this vocabulary learning strategy by having the class help you categorize the new vocabulary on the board in a chart or a mind map (using these headings).

- Finally, point out how to say you like a food or drink. Point to a photo (e.g., the pizza) and say as if you're eating and enjoying it, *Mmm, this pizza is delicious!* Then point to a different photo (e.g., the tea) and ask a student to say that the drink is good. Do the same with 3-4 different photos.

- After introducing the vocabulary in the Word Bank, tell students they are going to listen to a girl talk about the different photos on page 80. (If it helps, you can explain that the eight photos on page 80 are pictures the girl took of different foods and drinks.)

- Do the first one with the class. After you play the audio ask: *What photo does the girl talk about?* (Answer: *the one with the cereal, coffee, OJ, and fruit*). Tell students to write the number 1 on the photo. Then play the audio for items 2-8. At the end, check answers.

**Answers**
top row: 7, 4, 1   middle row: 8, 3, 5   bottom row: 6, 2

**E** 🔊 **Track 67** Read the sentences. Guess the answers. Then listen again. Write the word.

- Before students listen to the audio, tell them to read through sentences 1-8 and try to guess the answers. Tell them to think about what they heard in the audio and to use the photos (which they've numbered 1-8) to help them.

- Then play the audio and do the first one with the class. Ask for the answer that completes sentence one (Answer: *First, I need my coffee.*). Then play the rest of the audio and have students write a word in each blank for items 2-8. Pause the audio as needed so that students have time to write their answers.

**Answers**
1. coffee   2. pasta   3. pizza, third   4. tea   5. chicken, rice   6. ice cream   7. steak, fries   8. soup, salad

In sentence 8, the girl talks about her mom's homemade soup. Have students look at the word *homemade* (point out that it's made up of the words *home* and *made*). See if they can guess the meaning of the word. (Answer: If something is homemade, you cook (or make) it in your house. You don't buy it in the store.)

**EXPANSION** After students listen, have them take turns saying sentences 1-8 aloud with a partner.

**F** 🔁 What food and drinks on page 80 do you like? Circle them. Then ask a partner.

• Have students circle the food and drinks they like first. Go over the question and answers (about likes and dislikes) on page 81. Remind them that they learned this language in Unit 8. Then have students ask and answer about what they like and dislike from the food and drinks on page 80.

**ADDITIONAL VOCABULARY** On page 81, one person says *I don't eat meat.* Note for students that *meat* is food we get from animals, e.g., *beef* (like the steak that was mentioned), *chicken*, *pork* (like *ham* or *bacon*), and so on. A person who doesn't eat meat (or fish) is *vegetarian*.

**G** 🔁 Complete the sentences. Then say your sentences to a partner. Your partner asks a question.

• Tell students they already know the words for three kinds of drinks: *tea, coffee, juice.* In the Word Bank, there are three other drinks. Say the words *milk, soda,* and *water* with the class. Show a photo of each to clarify the meaning, or have students look the words up in their dictionaries.

• Next, have students work on their own to come up with three sentences about themselves. For each sentence, students should circle one of the words in blue and fill in the missing word(s).

• Finally, have students tell a partner each of their sentences. After each one, the partner should ask one question about it (as is modeled on the page).

**EXPANSION** Have students find a photo or two of a food or drink item on their phones. Project the following questions on the wall and have students work in pairs or small groups to answer them as they show their photo(s).

1. *What is the food or drink in the photo?*

2. *Do you like it?* (Use *It's good / delicious / OK.* or *No, not really* to explain.)

3. *When do you usually eat or drink it (for breakfast, lunch, dinner, dessert, or another time)?*

# 2 GRAMMAR

This Grammar lesson will focus on the word *some* and quantity expressions (*a bowl of, a cup of, a slice of,* and others) that are used to talk about amounts.

**A** 🔊 Track 68 Look at the pictures. Listen and repeat.

• Have students practice saying the words in the pictures to themselves first and then repeating after you. Point out that the /w/ is silent in the word *bowl.* Students can practice tapping out the syllables of each phrase on their desk, noting that the words in blue take the strongest stress.

• Play the audio and have students listen and repeat. Afterwards, have students cover the words and see if they can remember the phrase that goes with each picture.

1. *Cup* is frequently used with hot liquids, whereas *glass* is often used with cold or room temperature ones. In this lesson, students see *a cup of coffee/tea* and *a glass of milk/water/orange juice.* 2. *Slice* and *piece* sometimes overlap in usage. For example, it's possible to say both *a piece / slice of bread, pizza, pie, toast.* To keep things simple, in this lesson students see *a slice of bread/toast/pizza* vs. *a piece of cake/pie.* 3. We can put many things in a bowl or a bag, and sometimes, there's overlap in usage. For example, it's possible to talk about *a bowl of popcorn* or *a bag of popcorn.* To keep things simple, in this lesson, students see *a bowl of rice / pasta / soup / cereal* vs. *a bag of popcorn chips.*

**NOTICE** For the sake of simplicity, it's best to focus only on the quantity expression + noun combinations introduced in the lesson. If you want to share ways in which different quantity expressions can combine with the same noun (e.g., *a slice / piece of bread*), it's best to wait until after you have finished all of the Grammar exercises in the lesson. The game of concentration at the end of the lesson will not work properly if there is more than one possible answer for some items. Also, it will be less confusing if there is only one correct answer for each item.

**B** Study the chart.

> **LANGUAGE NOTE** This lesson focuses on how we use the phrase *a ___ of* to talk about a measureable amount of a noncount noun. (Nouncount nouns—such as *bread, cake,* and *water*—refer to a mass or an amount of something, occur in the singular, and are not preceded by *a/an*.) Sometimes *a ___ of* can be used with count nouns as well, but this lesson focuses on noncount nouns only and asking for portions of common foods.

> **LANGUAGE NOTE** The lesson also introduces *some*, which means "a certain amount" (when used with noncount nouns). It may be helpful to think of *some* as a plural form of *a/an*: *I want an orange. / I want some oranges. Some* can be used before plural count nouns (*oranges*) or noncount nouns (*fruit*), but again, in this lesson it will be used primarily with noncount nouns. The important point is that when students say *I want some water*, they are asking for an indefinite amount (as opposed to *I want a glass of water*, which specifies the amount).

- Have students read the sentences with *some* aloud: *I want some rice,* etc. Explain that *some* refers to a certain yet general amount: We don't know exactly how much.

- Next, have students look at the sentences using the pattern *a ___ of*. Explain that by using this expression, we are defining the amount of the whole that we want. While *some* coffee could refer to any amount, when you say *a cup of coffee* it's clear how much you are referring to.

- Have students close their books and take a survey. Read the words in random order and have students raise their hands. Ask *Who wants…?* (*a piece of cake, a cup of coffee,* etc.). Students can vote for as many of the items as they like (or none of the items, if they aren't hungry or thirsty). Tally the results and see which items are the most popular.

- Note: The word *of* is often reduced to a schwa sound /ə/ in expressions like *a cup of tea.* Students don't need to be taught to say it like that but they should be made aware that they may hear people pronounce it that way.

**C** Write the missing words.

- Have students work alone and write down their answers. Tell them that they can refer back to the grammar chart in **B** or clues when they are not sure of an answer.

**Answers**
1. a bowl of pasta   2. a bag of popcorn   3. a piece (slice) of pie   4. a bowl of cereal   5. a cup of tea   6. a slice (piece) of pizza   7. a glass of milk   8. a bowl of soup

**D** 🔁 Compare your answers in **C** with a partner's answers.

- Have students get into pairs and compare their answers. Go over the answers as a class.

- A fun way to go over the answers as a class is to ask one student at a time to draw an item on the board (e.g., a slice of pizza) without saying anything. When the student points at it, the other students should call out the answer. For this to work, students will have to draw the items in a random order.

**E** Will is home from school. Read the conversation. Guess the missing words.

- Go over the three new words in the Word Bank. Draw a timeline on the board with the times 12:00, 4:00, and 6:30 marked on it. Write the word *lunch* next to 12:00 and *dinner* next to 6:30. Then write the word *now* next to 4:00. Say *Dinner is at 6:30* (rubbing your stomach and licking your lips). *It's 4:00 now. And I'm hungry now. I want a snack.* Explain that a snack is a small portion of food, usually eaten between regular meals. When do students usually have a snack? In the morning, afternoon, or evening? Take a class poll.

- Ask students what kinds of snacks they have. Write their answers on the board. (Possible answers include: candy, nuts, fruit, popcorn, pizza, cheese and crackers, and chips.) Point at an item such as *fruit* and say *This is a healthy snack.* Point at *candy* and say *This is not a healthy snack.*

**EXPANSION** Put students into pairs. Ask each pair to come up with one healthy and one unhealthy snack. Have everyone share their answers with the class.

- Give students time to read through the conversation silently and ask you any questions about vocabulary. Make sure they understand all of the words (e.g., *in an hour*). Have students temporarily close their books and ask some comprehension questions:

*What time is dinner?* (5:30) *What does Will want?* (a snack)
*What time is it now?* (4:30) *How does Will feel?* (He's hungry.)

- Next give them some time to guess the missing words in the conversation. They can think about the possible answers or they can write down their guesses lightly in pencil next to the blanks. If time allows, put students into pairs to compare their guesses.

**F** 🔊 **Track 69** Listen to the conversation in **E**. Check your answers.

- Play the audio and have students check their answers.

- To go over the answers, split the class in half. One half of the students will read the part of "Will," while the other half will play the role of "Mom." Read the dialogue with the students in unison with the "Will" students reading aloud when you are on his lines and the "Mom" students chiming in on Mom's lines.

- After reading through the answers together, ask individual students to come to the board and write down the sentences that contain missing words. Correct any spelling errors at this point.

**Answers**

Will: Mom, can I have a snack?
Mom: Will, it's 4:30 now. Dinner is in an hour.
Will: But, Mom, I'm hungry!
Mom: OK. Do you want a piece of <u>fruit</u>? We have some oranges.
Will: No, I want some <u>ice cream</u>.

Mom: No, Will, that's for dessert.
Will: OK, can I have some <u>chips</u>?
Mom: No, that's not healthy. Eat a small bowl of <u>soup</u>, or drink a glass of <u>juice</u>.
Will: OK.

**G** ✏️ Write your own conversation. Use **E** as a model. Say it with a partner.

- Put students into pairs and tell them that they are going to write their own conversations. Tell them that their conversation should include the following expressions:
*Can I have a snack?*
*I'm hungry!* OR *Are you hungry?*
*Do you want...?*
*We have some...*

**PRONUNCIATION TIP**

Remind students that *can* usually becomes /kən/ in the affirmative and the interrogative (The vowel sound is reduced):
*Can I have a snack?*
*You can have a piece of fruit.*

**ADDITIONAL VOCABULARY** Provide additional vocabulary that they may need for their conversations. (For example, helping students with language for how to refuse a suggestion—*No, thanks. I don't want that.*)

- Students should use the conversation in **E** for ideas but they don't have to follow it exactly. Tell them to be creative! Circulate and assist with language as necessary.

- Once students have finished, have them practice their conversations with their partners. They should take turns playing each of the roles in the conversation.

- Finally, invite some students to come to the front of the room and perform their conversations. At the end of each conversation ask students to tell you which foods or drinks were mentioned and which ones the person accepted or refused.

**H** 🎲 Read the instructions. Work in a group. Play the game.

- This is a game of concentration.

**NOTE** For this game to work properly, there can only be one correct answer for each collocation. (That is, while it may be possible to say *a piece of pizza* we are only accepting *a slice of pizza* as the correct answer in this game.)

- Review the different collocations (answers are below) with the class before you start the game. You can do this by writing the food and drink words (*popcorn*, *coffee*, etc.) and then calling out an expression like *a bag of,* and students have to then complete it (with the answer of *chips* or *popcorn*). Before you start the game, erase them.

**PREP WORK** Prepare a set of 24 blank slips of paper (of uniform size) for each group that will be playing the game. Alternatively, have the students cut out the slips of paper themselves if there is time.

- To prepare to play the game, each group of students should write each of the expressions listed in chart 1 on separate pieces of paper. They should write each of the six expressions twice for a total of 12 pieces of paper.

- They should then write each of the 12 words listed in chart 2 on the remaining 12 pieces of paper.

**CLASSROOM MANAGEMENT** Assign students in each group a task (e.g., one student writes the words from the first column in chart 1 twice) to help them organize their prep work.

- Then have them shuffle the 24 pieces of paper thoroughly. They should then place the papers face down in six rows of four.

- The first student to go will then choose two random papers to turn over. If they match (e.g., the student turns over *a slice of* and *pizza*) then the student picks up the papers, says *A slice of pizza: It's a match*, and removes the papers. That student then gets to take another turn.

- The same player keeps turning over papers until he/she turns over two papers that don't match (e.g., *a cup of* and *pizza*). When papers don't match, the student should turn them back over and it's the next student's turn. Tell the students that even if they don't make a match right away, they should still pay careful attention because the winner will be the person in later rounds who can remember the location of certain papers.

- Keep playing in this way until all the matches have been made. The student with the most matches is the winner. Students can play several rounds if they like and rotate so that they play with different students.

**Answers**
There are 12 matches in the game.
a bag of chips / a bag of popcorn
a bowl of cereal / a bowl of rice
a cup of coffee / a cup of tea
a piece of fruit / a piece of pie
a glass of milk / a glass of orange juice
a slice of bread / a slice of pizza

# 3 SPEAKING

In this Speaking lesson, students will practice ordering and paying for food and drinks.

**A** Look at the photo. Answer the questions with a partner.

- Look at the photo on the page and tell students to read the caption. Then ask: *Where is this food truck? What food does it sell?* Then have students discuss the questions on the page with a partner. Discuss answers with the class.

**CULTURE NOTE** Food trucks are common in many countries and have recently become very popular in cities in the US. A food truck is a type of large vehicle (like the one pictured) in which food is prepared and then sold on the street. Food trucks often specialize in a specific type of food (e.g., ice cream, sandwiches, noodle dishes), and the items sold are usually inexpensive.

**B** Say the sentences in the Useful Language box with your teacher.

- Explain to students that they are going to learn to order (ask for) and pay for food and drink, as you would at a food truck, in a restaurant, a coffee shop, etc. Say the sentences in the Useful Language box with the class, and help students notice the points in the Language Note below.

**LANGUAGE NOTE**

1. *I'd like = I would like*. It means *I want* and is used to make a polite request.

2. When we order a main dish or item, it's common to use *I'd like the...* (e.g., *I'd like the chicken sandwich. I'd like the pasta.*) With drinks, we tend to use *a/an* (e.g., *I'd like an iced tea*), but with *water,* it's more common to say *a bottle of water*. (See the Notice! note on page 85.)

3. When we ask for or order something, it's more polite to use the word *please*.

4. *That's...* is often used to say how much a person must pay (*That's six fifty.*). Note how the price is said in US dollars.

5. When we give or hand something to someone, it's common to say *Here you go.* or just *Here.* Model this for the class by pretending to give your pen to a student.

**C** Track 70 Read and listen to the conversation.

- Before students do this exercise, do the following:
  Point to the menu on the facing page and say the word *menu* with the class.

- Tell students to look at the menu. (The woman in the dialogue orders from this menu.) Review these words with students; if possible show photos to illustrate their meanings: *plate, sandwich, taco, iced* (cold) *tea.*

- Note that *Extras* (listed on the menu) often refer to smaller items (sometimes called *sides*) that you can order with your main dish.

- After you've done this, have students read the dialogue to themselves silently. Then play the audio once through. For additional practice, play the audio again. At the end, ask students: *What does the woman order?*

**D** 🔄 Work with a partner. Say the conversation in **C**.

- Have students work in pairs to practice the conversation in **C**. After they've done it once, have them change roles and practice again.

**E** 🔄 Work with a partner. Say the conversation in **C** again. Order from the menu.

- Have students substitute information from the menu in the dialogue. Tell them to order one main item, one extra, and a drink. (When they order their drink, they should pay attention to the information in the Notice! note.) The server will have to total the new cost for the order and ask for it. Model this once for the class with a student volunteer.

**F** 🔄 Change roles. Repeat **E**.

- Have students change roles. Encourage the person ordering to choose different items this time.

**G** 🔄 Work with a partner. Make your own food truck.

- Working in pairs, students should come up with ideas for their own food truck and give it a name. They can go with an idea on the page or come up with their own (e.g., a truck that serves different types of barbequed (BBQ) meat, or one that serves fruit popsicles). Encourage students to be creative, and assist with vocabulary as needed.

- On their menus, students should list five or six items with prices, ensuring that all is easy to see at a distance. (Other students will be reading and selecting items from their menus.) When each pair has finished, they should post their menus on one of their desks or on the wall behind them.

**H** 🎲 Get into two groups (A and B).

- In each pair, assign students the role of A or B. In this round, all Student A's should stay at their desk with their menu taking people's orders. All Student B's will circulate, visiting different food trucks and ordering food. Student B's should record their orders in the chart on the page.

**SUPPORT** Tell students they can use the dialogue in **C** for help but that they should try to do the exercise as much as possible without reading directly from their books.

**I** 🎲 Change roles. Repeat **H**.

- In this round, Student A's will visit the food trucks and Student B's will stay at their desks with their menus and ask for people's orders.

**J** 🔄 Talk about your orders with a partner. Use the sentence.

- Have students tell a partner about the items they ordered using the sentence provided on the page. Note that the word *ordered* is the past tense of the verb *order.*

# PUT IT TOGETHER 4

## 1 GRAMMAR

This Grammar lesson will review the four kinds of question types students have learned up to this point:

1) *Yes / No* questions with *be* (*Put it Together* 1)

2) *Yes / No* questions with other verbs (*Put it Together* 2)

3) *Wh-* questions with *be* (*Put it Together* 3)

4) *Wh-* questions with other verbs (Unit 11)

Note: Unlike previous review units, *Put it Together 4* contains language not only from Units 10-12 but also from other (earlier) units in the book.

**A** Read the questions. Match a picture with a question.

- For this first exercise, students will review the meanings of the four question words (*who, what, where, when*) and get some practice with *Wh-* questions (using the verb *be* and other verbs). This is a quick way to see where students may be struggling with question forms.

- Read each of the four questions aloud with students. Then ask them to study the pictures and (working alone) match each question to a photo. Go over the answers as a class.

- Have students work in pairs to come up with two different answers of their own to each question. (The answers all require students to use language they've learned from previous units.)

**SUPPORT** To help students with this task, you can remind them that *who* is used for people, *what* for information, *when* for dates and times, and *where* for place. Possible answers to the four questions: (Note: Both short and full answers should be accepted.)

1. Q: Who do you live with? A: (I live with) my family / my mother, father, and brother.

2. Q: What do you do on the weekend? A: I go shopping / go to the gym.

3. Q: When is your birthday? A: (My birthday is) on May 17th / (My birthday is) in May / in the winter.

4. Q: Where is your hometown? A: (My hometown is) in Argentina / near (city name) / in (name of province or area).

**Answers**
1C  2A  3B  4D

**B** Complete the questions. Write the missing question words.

- Have students review the words and phrases from the exercise (e.g., *summer vacation*, *neighborhood*, etc.) and make sure they understand their meanings.

**CHALLENGE** If appropriate in your institution, call out different vocabulary words and phrases from the exercise and have students give you their meanings in their native language.

- Give students time to fill in the missing question words. Tell them to put their pencils/pens down when they're finished. Then ask different volunteers to come to the board and write out one of the questions (until all seven of them are up on the board). Then go over the questions together as a class.

Notes: 1. If item #4 is too intrusive, have students skip it or they can make up an answer. 2. Both *where* and *when* are possible answers for item #6. You don't need to tell this to students ahead of time. It might be interesting to see what they come up with!

**Answers**
1. <u>What</u> do you watch on TV?   2. <u>When</u> is summer vacation?   3. <u>Where</u> do you buy food in your neighborhood?   4. <u>What</u> does your father do?
5. <u>Who</u> do you live with?   6. <u>Where / When</u> do you go to school?   7. <u>What</u> is your nickname?

**C** 🔁 Work with a partner. Ask and answer the questions in **B**.

- Read the example with a student, then have a student ask you the next question. Put students in pairs. Have them take turns asking and answering the questions from **B**. Circulate around the room and assist as necessary.

**EXPANSION** Have each pair choose one of the questions and an appropriate answer and build a short conversation around it. (Note: Students should change the language slightly if they need to.)

**SUPPORT** Write one or more of the conversations on the board or project them with the underlined information missing. Students can then use one of the conversations as a model, filling in the missing information with their own ideas.

- Here are some possible conversations that students might come up with.

A: What do you watch on TV?
B: I like (name of show).
A: I don't like that show.
B: Really? It's my favorite. What's your favorite show?
A: I like (name of show).

A: Who do you live with?
B: My sister, Alina.
A: Where do you live?
B: We live in (name of place).

A: This is a picture of my family.
B: Who is that?
A: That's my mother.
B: What does she do?
A: She's a businesswoman.

A: Hi, I'm Alexandra. But please call me Alex.
B: Hi, Alex. I'm Janet.
A: What's your nickname, Janet?
B: It's Jan.
A: Well, it's nice to meet you.
B: Nice to meet you, too.

- Some students can perform their conversations for the class.

**D** Study the charts.

- This is a lot of material, but remember that it is all a review of language students have seen before.
- Start with the first chart, *Yes / No* and *Wh-* questions with *be*. Read the statement (*I am Peruvian.*) together as a class.

**LANGUAGE NOTE** Point out that in the *Yes / No* question, the subject and verb change places in the sentence. (It may be helpful to draw arrows on the chart showing this switch.)

- Go over the responses (*Yes, I am / No, I'm not*) as well. Then ask different individual students this question with different nationalities: *Are you Peruvian? Are you Dominican? Are you British?* etc. and have them answer.

**PREP WORK** Come to class with several pictures of famous people and ask the class different questions about the people:

(The royal family in England) *Are they French? Are they British? Are they students?*
(Taylor Swift) *Is she Australian? Is she American? Is she a singer?*
(Cristiano Ronaldo) *Is he Spanish? Is he Portuguese? Is he a soccer player?*

The important thing here (and with all the question forms) is that you give students practice with different pronoun forms so that they are not only answering questions that feature the pronoun *you.*

- Continue on with the *Wh-* question with *be.*

**LANGUAGE NOTE** In the same way, point out that the subject and verb switch places from the statement to the question form. Practice asking and answering the question in the chart and then use the same pictures of famous people to ask *Where is he/she from?* or *Where are they from?* Students can give either the short or long answers.

**LANGUAGE NOTE** Moving on to the second chart (*Yes / No* and *Wh-* Questions with Other Verbs), there are two important things to mention: 1. the subject and verb do not switch position between statements and the question form, and 2. you have to insert *do* or *does* to make the question form.

- Go over the statement and questions in the second chart. Have students use their own local information to ask and answer the two questions with a partner: *Do you live in* (name of city)? *Where do you live exactly?* After that, you can once again ask your students questions about the famous people.

**E** Write questions. Follow the pattern.

- Go over the meaning of the word *dish,* used here to mean "food prepared in a particular way" by asking students to name some dishes that are representative of their country. (You can do this by saying, *"Paella" is a famous dish in Spain. What are some famous dishes you know?*)

- Tell students that they should use the letter prompts to form four different questions about food. Give them some time to work and then go over their answers as a class by having some students write their answers on the board. Make sure everyone understands the different meanings of the questions *What dishes do you like?* (asking in general; plural form) and *What is your favorite food?* (asking for specifics; singular form). Note that while a *dish* is something prepared with multiple ingredients, typically eaten as a main course (e.g., a casserole or a pasta dish), a *favorite food* can refer to something that takes time to prepare (e.g., a cake) or even a simple food (e.g., broccoli or melon).

**Answers**
1. What dishes do you like?    2. What is your favorite food?
3. Do you like pasta?    4. Is your favorite food pasta?

**F** 🔄 Ask your partner the questions in **E**. Write his or her answers in your notebook.

- Put students into pairs and have them ask and answer the questions from **E**. Circulate and help students with vocabulary as necessary.

**CLASSROOM MANAGEMENT** Skip the step of having students write down their partners' answers if time is limited.

**EXPANSION** After each pair has finished, ask them to join another pair. Each student should then introduce his or her partner to the group: *This is Jae-Hwa. She likes pasta with tomato sauce and Korean barbecue. Her favorite food is kimchee...*

**G** Write the questions. Put the words in order.

- In this exercise, students will be unscrambling the sentences to form questions. First make sure they understand the expression *go out to dinner*. Draw a picture of a house on the board and as you mimic eating, saying *eat dinner at home*. Then draw an arrow out from the house and say *go out to dinner*. Ask the class *Do you sometimes go out to dinner?* Have students vote by raising their hands. Ask, *Where do you go?*

- Give students time to unscramble the sentences. There are ten of them, so it may be helpful to assign students to work in pairs.

**CLASSROOM MANAGEMENT** To save time, assign each pair a letter (A – E) and tell each pair to do only two items: Pair A should do items 1-2, Pair B items 3-4, and so on. At the end of the activity, all students

should listen closely while other pairs are reporting their answers and write them in their books. They will need to have all the answers written down in order to complete the following exercise.

**Answers**
1. Are you free after school?    2. What do you have for breakfast?    3. What is your teacher's name?
4. Do you go to bed early?    5. Is your English class fun?    6. When does school start?    7. Are your parents over 50?    8. Does your family go out for dinner?
9. Where is your school? 10. Does your favorite singer sing in English?

**H** Match the questions in **G** to their answers below.

- If you have students working in pairs, they can remain with their partners and complete the next exercise. Give them time to match the answers to the questions in **G**. Go over the answers by having one student stand and read a question from **G** and then choose another student to stand and answer it correctly.

**Answers**
7a  2b  10c  9d  5e  6f  8g  1h  4i  3j

**I** 🔄 Work with a partner. Write a conversation. Use a question from **G** in your conversation.

- Students will now work in pairs, making a short conversation that includes a question from **G**. You should explain to them that the question can start things off or it can come in the middle or at the end of the conversation. Tell them that they should make the conversation long enough so that it goes on for at least 30 seconds. Point out the conversation in **J** to show students how the exercise will work. Encourage students to be creative and funny.

- After they finish writing out their conversation, give them time to practice it a few times, using the read and look up method.

**J** 👥 Find another pair. Say your conversation.

- Put two pairs together and have them perform their conversations for each other. The goal is to give students enough practice so that they are becoming less and less reliant on the written word and committing more of the conversation to memory. Circulate and help students with language as necessary.

**EXPANSION** Have some pairs come to the front of the class and perform their conversations. At the end, have students vote with applause for their favorite one.

# 2 SEE IT AND SAY IT

**A** Look at the picture. What food and drink do you see? Write the quantities and the words.

- Give students a moment to study the picture. Project the picture on a screen or a wall and have individual students come to the front of the room and identify one item at a time. Another option is to put students into pairs and have them take turns identifying items. Point to the following items in the picture and teach the additional vocabulary: balloons, jacket, scarf, and can.

- Go over the first answer with the students. Then give them some time to identify the other five items they see. They can work in pairs if necessary.

**Answers**
1. a bowl of ice cream   2. a piece/slice of cake
3. a bottle of water   4. a piece/slice of pizza
5. a bag of chips   6. a can of soda

**B** Read the sentences about the picture in **A**. Circle *True* or *False*. Rewrite the false sentences to make them true.

- Do the first item together to show the students how the exercise works. Give them 5 minutes to work silently. They should study the picture for clues and circle true or false. For the false sentences, they should rewrite them to make them true.

- Read each sentence aloud and on the count of three, have students call out True or False. Then ask several students to write the sentences that they rewrote on the board. Correct any errors.

**Answers**
1. False; It's a birthday party.   2. False; The party is for Mei.
3. False; It's fall.   4. True   5. False; The party is in November.   6. False; The party is at eight o'clock.

# 3 WHAT DO YOU USUALLY DO ON YOUR BIRTHDAY?

**A** Read the conversations. Guess the answers.

- Read each line of the conversations, pausing to give students time to repeat after you. (For the blanks in the conversation, you can clap your hands once. Students should do the same.)

- Give students some time to work alone and guess the missing words. Ask different students to volunteer some of their ideas.

**B** 🔊 Track 71  Listen. Complete the conversations in **A**.

- Have students listen and complete the conversations. Then go over the answers as a class.

**EXPANSION** Put students into pairs and have them practice one or both of the conversations. They each get a chance to play both roles (A and B).

**Answers**
Conversation 1: big, Monday, good
Conversation 2: dinner, home, ice cream

**C** ⚡ Ask a partner. What do you usually do on your birthday?

- Put students into pairs. Have them ask their partners the question *What do you usually do on your birthday?* Tell them to listen for the answer and then to try and ask at least one follow-up question.

- Make three columns on the board and write these words at the top of each one: *I eat… / I go… / I ____*. Point to the first column and have students call out some of the things that they eat on their birthdays (e.g., *cake* or *ice cream*). Make a list. Then do the same thing for the second column; have students call out any places that they go to on their birthdays (e.g., *go to the movies* or *go out to dinner*). For the third column, leave it open for any other answers that the students might have (e.g., *stay home* or *have a party*). Take a poll and see if any of the items on the board match more than one student in the class. Are there any popular birthday foods or birthday destinations shared by the students in the class?

# 4 THE QUESTION GAME

In this activity, students will review asking and answering *Yes / No* and *Wh-* questions with the verb *be* and other verbs.

**A** Read the questions below. If your answer is *yes*, put a check (✓) in the *Me* column.

- Point out the *do you* questions in the left-hand column of the chart. Give students an opportunity to practice asking and answering them. Start with one student (Student A) and have him/her ask the first question (*Do you get up late on the weekend*) to the student sitting directly behind him/her (Student B). B should answer the question and then ask the next question (*Do you always eat breakfast*) to the next student (C). Continue this way until you've worked your way around the entire class so that each student has had a chance to both ask and answer a question. Correct any errors as they arise.

- Then have students read each of the eight questions and think about themselves. If their own answer to a question is *yes*, they should put a checkmark (✓) next to it in the "Me" column. If their answer is *no*, they should leave it blank. When students are finished, ask them to put their pen/pencil down and look up.

- Now have students look at the column on the right-hand side of the chart that lists *Wh-* question words. Brainstorm with students possible questions that they could ask as follow-up questions after the *do you* questions. There's no need to spend a lot of time on this; just go through it quickly so that students get a rough idea of what they will be doing in the exercise. Answers for possible follow-up questions:

  1. *Do you get up late on the weekend? When do you get up?*
  2. *Do you always eat breakfast? What do you eat?*
  3. *Do you do homework after school? Where do you do your homework?* (notice *your*)
  4. *Do you see friends on the weekend? Who do you see?*
  5. *Do you have an older sister? What's her name?*
  6. *Do you live near school? Where do you live (exactly)?*
  7. *Do you like hip hop music? Who is your favorite artist/singer?* OR *Who do you listen to?*
  8. *Do you have a birthday in the spring? When is your birthday (exactly)?*

**B** 👥 Talk to different classmates. Complete the chart in A.

- For this part of the exercise, students need to stand and move about the classroom. They are going to talk to their classmates and try to find other students that answered *yes* to the *do you* questions.

- When you call out "Go!" a student (e.g., Student A) should approach a classmate (Student B) and ask a *do you* question from the chart. If Student B answers *yes* to the question A should write down his/her classmate's name and ask a follow-up question. A should listen to B's response and also write it down. Model the activity with one or two questions before students begin.

- A student wins the game by filling up his/her chart first with names of his/her classmates and their answers and then sitting down. Make a note of the order that the students finish in and allow the game to continue for as long as you can. Once the game has ended, go back to the student who finished first and have him/her share his/her answers. If all of the information is correct, that student is declared the winner. If there are any discrepancies in his/her answers, move on to the next student and check his/her answers. Keep doing this until you have a winner. If you have time, have other students share their answers with the class too.

**NOTICE** There are some rules that make the game more interesting: 1. It's a race, so students should try and fill up their chart as fast as they can. 2. Tell students that they cannot use a student's name for more than one of the items on the chart. For example, they can't just stand and ask one student all eight questions and then write his/her name next to six of them (if he/she answers *yes*). Students need to circulate around the room and talk to different students. 3. Although the game is a race, students still need to be polite. Once they've asked their question, they need to give their partner an opportunity to ask a question as well so that everyone gets a chance at winning. In other words, students can't simply race about the room asking questions without answering anyone's questions.

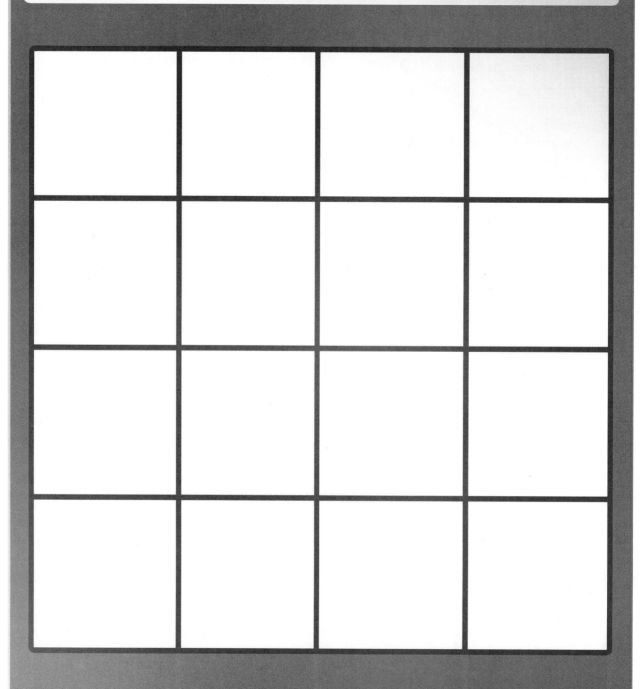

# LANGUAGE SUMMARIES

## UNIT **1** CLASSROOM INSTRUCTIONS

| | | | |
|---|---|---|---|
| answer (the question) | **Word Bank** | **Grammar** | **Speaking** |
| ask (your teacher) | yes | Listen to the conversation. | Good morning / afternoon / evening. |
| circle (the word) | no | | |
| close (your book) | please | Open your books. | Can you repeat that? / Can you say that again? |
| cover (the page) | numbers 1–5 | | |
| listen (and repeat) | | | |
| look at (the picture) | | | |
| open (your book) | | | |
| read (the sentence) | | | |
| say (the word) | | | |
| write (your name) | | | |

## UNIT **2** MY NAME IS...

| | | | |
|---|---|---|---|
| Letters of the alphabet (A-Z) | **Word Bank** | **Grammar** | **Speaking** |
| | Mr. / Ms. | I'm a student. | Hello. / Hi. |
| businessman/woman | | You're a student. | I'm Aya. / My name is Aya. |
| doctor | | She's a teacher. | |
| programmer | | | (It's) nice to meet you (too). |
| soccer player | | | |
| student | | | |
| teacher | | | |

# UNIT 3 OUR CLASSROOM

backpack

(white)board

bookcase

chair

clock

(laptop) computer

desk

dictionary

door

eraser

map

notebook

pen

pencil

phone

screen

table

textbook

umbrella

window

this / these

## Word Bank

ID card

## Grammar

What's this? / It's an eraser.

What are these? / They're pencils.

## Speaking

Can I use your phone?

Sure.

Thanks. / Thank you.

You're welcome. / No problem.

# PUT IT TOGETHER 1

## Word Bank

I don't know.

## Grammar

Am I in this class? / Yes, you are. No, you're not.

Are you a student? / Yes, I am. No, I'm not.

Is she a teacher? / Yes, she is. No, she's not.

Are they students? / Yes, they are. No, they're not.

# UNIT 4 PERSONAL INFORMATION

**Numbers 1–20 & 0**

student ID number

email address

phone number

What's your email address / phone number?

It's...

**Word Bank**

@ = at

.com = dot com

.edu = dot e-d-u

.net = dot net

(best) friend

different

new

Sorry!

Yeah.

**Grammar**

Your ID number is 16.

Her phone number is 555–2436.

Its name is Maru.

This is our class.

**Speaking**

Hello?

Hi, it's Max.

Excuse me, who's calling?

# UNIT 5 MY NEIGHBORHOOD

ATM

bank

bus stop

cafe / coffee shop

gym

movie theater

park

post office

restaurant

school

store

supermarket

neighborhood

car

garage

tree

**Word Bank**

bookstore

clothing store

department store

favorite

street

**Grammar**

There's an ATM on my street.

There are no / two / some stores in my neighborhood.

**Speaking**

Excuse me. Is there a gym near here?

Go straight. Turn left / right on Jay Street.

Sorry, I don't know.

neighborhood

Australia / Australian

Brazil / Brazilian

Canada / Canadian

China / Chinese

Japan / Japanese

Korea / Korean

Mexico / Mexican

Peru / Peruvian

Portugal / Portuguese

Spain / Spanish

Sweden / Swedish

the United Kingdom / British

the United States / American

Turkey / Turkish

Venezuela / Venezuelan

Vietnam / Vietnamese

in (+ city / country)

beautiful

big

exciting

old

small

## Word Bank

flag

French

language

soup

actor

famous

food

fun

interesting

near

## Grammar

New York is interesting.

New York is an interesting city.

## Speaking

Where are you from?

(I'm from) China.

Where in China?

Suzhou. It's near Shanghai.

My city is famous for its parks. / New York City is famous for Central Park.

# PUT IT TOGETHER **2**

## Word Bank

flight

job

## Grammar

Who is she? / (She's) my friend.

What is it? / (It's) a computer.

Where are they? / (They're) in Lima.

# UNIT 7  FAMILY

mother (mom)

father (dad)

(older / younger) sister

(older / younger) brother

grandmother

grandfather

aunt

uncle

cousin

parents

grandparents

Numbers 21-100

**Word Bank**

a lot of

free time

(have) homework

husband

on vacation

wife

**Grammar**

I have a big family.

He has short hair.

We have a lot of friends.

**Speaking**

You look like your sister. / You look like her.

How old are you?

I'm 19.

# UNIT 8  MY FAVORITES

funny

popular

sad

scary

dance

hip hop

pop

rock

play video games

read comic books

watch movies

**Word Bank**

band/group

club

singer

song

**Grammar**

I like / She likes hip hop.

I don't like / She doesn't like hip hop.

**Speaking**

Do you like rock?

Yes, I love it! / Yeah, it's OK. / No, not really.

# UNIT 9  TIME

**What time is it?**

It's three o'clock.
/ It's three oh five. / It's three ten.

It's three fifteen.
/ It's three thirty.

It's three forty-five.
/ It's three fifty. / It's three fifty-five.

noon

midnight

at (+ time)

computer club

drama club

English club

swim practice

band practice

have an appointment

have a test

have class / swim practice

**Word Bank**

art

history

math

P.E.

science

lunch

break

reservation

test

go shopping

shoes

**Grammar**

When is English class?

It's at 2:00.

It's in the morning / afternoon / evening.

It's before / after math.

It's now / later / today / tomorrow.

**Speaking**

Let's go shopping.

(That) sounds great. / (Sorry,) I can't. I have class.

Are you free at 2:00 / later / in the morning?

Yes. / Yeah. / No. I have class.

# PUT IT TOGETHER 3

| Word Bank | Grammar |
| --- | --- |
| pet | Do you like math? / Yes, I do. No, I don't. |
| difficult | Does he read comic books? / Yes, he does. No, he doesn't. |
| homeroom | Do they have homework? / Yes, they do. No, they don't. |
| invite | |

# UNIT 10 MY ROUTINE

get up

check my text messages

take a shower

get dressed

go to school

start/finish (school)

go home

do homework

go to bed


Days of the week


on (+ day of the week)

go (+ verb + *ing*)

go (+ *to* + place)

### Word Bank

routine


choose

early

late

miss (class)

nervous

### Grammar

He is always / usually / often / sometimes / never late.

She always / usually / often / sometimes / never gets up early.

### Speaking

What do you usually do on the weekend?

Not much. I get up late. Sometimes I see my friends.

I'm really busy. I have a class on Saturday morning.

# UNIT 11 IMPORTANT DAYS

Months of the year


Ordinal numbers 1st – 31st


in (+ month)

on (+ date)

by (+ *bus / car*)

### Word Bank

birthday


What do you do?


have a party

check in

buy

serve

wear

New Year's Day

New Year's Eve


film festival

food festival

last

Seasons of the year

### Grammar

Where do you live? / (I live) in Santiago.

When do they study? / (They study) in April.

How does she go to school? (She goes to school) by bus.

### Speaking

When is the Halloween party?

It's this Saturday.

I'm not sure. Is it on Saturday?

I don't know. / I have no idea.

# UNIT 12 FOOD

bread

cereal

chicken

coffee

fries

fruit

ice cream

orange juice

pasta

pizza

rice

salad

soup

steak

tea

bread

cake

chips

pie

popcorn

## Word Bank

breakfast / lunch / dinner

dessert

eat

drink

milk

soda

water

delicious

good

healthy

hungry

snack

## Grammar

I want some rice.

I want a bowl of rice / a cup of coffee / a slice of bread.

I want a glass of water / a piece of cake / a bag of chips.

## Speaking

I'd like the chicken sandwich, (please).

Anything else?

A bag of chips, (please). / No thanks.

That's $6.50.

Here you go.

# PUT IT TOGETHER 4

## Word Bank
dish

## Grammar
Are you Peruvian? / Yes, I am. No, I'm not.

Where are you from? / (I'm from) Peru.

Do you live in Tokyo? / Yes, I do. No, I'm don't.

Where do you live exactly? / (I live in) Nezu.

# UNIT 1

### Page 2, Vocabulary, Exercise A (Track 2)

1. listen
2. say
3. read
4. write
5. ask
6. answer
7. circle
8. cover
9. open
10. close
11. look
12. repeat

### Page 4, Grammar, Exercise A (Track 3)

1. book
2. conversation
3. teacher
4. page
5. name
6. picture
7. question
8. sentence
9. word

### Page 4, Grammar, Exercise C (Track 4)

1. Answer the question.
2. Open your book.
3. Cover the page.
4. Read the sentence.
5. Listen to the conversation.
6. Write your name.
7. Look at the picture.
8. Listen and repeat.
9. Say the word.
10. Close your book.
11. Circle the word.
12. Raise your hand.

### Page 6, Speaking, Exercise B (Track 5)

Teacher: Good morning, everyone. Please open your books to page five.

Student: Emily?

Teacher: Yes?

Student: Can you repeat that?

Teacher: Yes. Open to page five.

### Page 7, Speaking, Exercise D (Track 6)

*Conversation 1*

Teacher: Good afternoon, everyone. Please open your books to page three.

Student: Emily? Can you say that again?

Teacher: Yes, open to page three.

*Conversation 2*

Teacher: Good morning, everyone. Please open your books to page five.

Student: Emily? Can you repeat that?

Teacher: Yes, open to page five.

# UNIT 2

### Page 8, Vocabulary, Exercise A (Track 7)

*Letters of the Alphabet*

Aa Bb Cc Dd Ee Ff Gg Hh Ii Jj
Kk Ll Mm Nn Oo Pp Qq Rr Ss
Tt Uu Vv Ww Xx Yy Zz

### Page 9, Vocabulary, Exercise D (Track 8)

1. I'm Pedro. P-E-D-R-O.
2. I'm Mahesh. M-A-H-E-S-H.
3. I'm Lily. L-I-L-Y.
4. I'm Jacob. J-A-C-O-B.
5. I'm Olivia. O-L-I-V-I-A.

### Page 10, Grammar, Exercise C (Track 9)

1. I am a student.
2. You are a teacher.
3. He is a soccer player.
4. She is a doctor.
5. He is a businessman.
6. She is a programmer.

## Page 10, Grammar, Exercise D (Track 10)

1. I'm a student.

2. You're a teacher.

3. He is a soccer player.

4. She is a doctor.

5. He's a businessman.

6. She's a programmer.

## Page 12, Speaking, Exercise B (Track 11)

A:   Hello. I'm Lisa.

B:   Hi, Lisa. My name is Tomas.

A:   Nice to meet you.

B:   Nice to meet you, too.

## Page 13, Speaking, Exercise F (Track 12)

*Conversation 1*

A:   Hi. My name is Aya.

B:   Hello, Aya. I'm Leo.

A:   Nice to meet you.

B:   Nice to meet you, too.

*Conversation 2*

A:   Hi, I'm Marc.

B:   Hi, Marc. I'm Paula.

A:   Nice to meet you.

B:   You, too.

# UNIT 3

## Page 15, Vocabulary, Exercise A (Track 13)

a. backpack

b. door

c. (white)board

d. chair

e. pen

f. clock

g. (laptop) computer

h. notebook

i. desk

j. dictionary

k. bookcase

l. eraser

m. map

n. screen

o. table

p. textbook

q. pencil

r. phone

s. umbrella

t. window

## Page 16, Grammar, Exercise D (Track 14)

1. What's this? It's a backpack.

2. What is this? It is a backpack.

## Page 16, Grammar, Exercise E (Track 15)

1. What is this? It's a map.

2. What's this? It's a bookcase.

3. What's this? It is a textbook.

4. What's this? It's a laptop.

## Page 18, Speaking, Exercise B (Track 16)

A:   Can I use your pen?

B:   Sure.

A:   Thanks.

B:   You're welcome.

## Page 18, Speaking, Exercise E (Track 17)

*Conversation 1*

A:   Can I use your pen?

B:   Sure.

A:   Thank you.

B:   You're welcome.

*Conversation 2*

A:   Can I use your pen?

B:   Sure.

A:   Thanks.

B:   No problem.

# PUT IT TOGETHER 1

## Page 20, Grammar, Exercise D (Track 18)

*Conversation 1*

A:   What's this?

B:   I don't know. Is it a laptop?

*Conversation 2*

A:   Is he a teacher?

B:   I don't know. Maybe.

*Conversation 3*

A:   What are these?

B:   I don't know. Are they maps?

## Page 23, Listening, Exercise B (Track 19)

*Conversation 1*

A:   Hi, I'm Alex.

B:   Hi, Alex. My name is Hector.

A:   Hector. Can you spell that, please?

B:   Sure. It's H-E-C-T-O-R.

A:    Oh, OK. Got it. Nice to meet you, Hector.

B:    Nice to meet you, too!

*Conversation 2*

A:    Can I use your phone?

B:    Sure, no problem.

A:    Thank you!

B:    You're welcome.

*Conversation 3*

A:    Good morning, class.

B:    Good morning, Mr. Lee.

A:    Please open your books. (pause) OK, listen and repeat.What's this?

B:    What's this?

# UNIT 4
### Page 24, Vocabulary, Exercise A (Track 20)

| | | |
|---|---|---|
| Zero. | Seven. | Fourteen. |
| One. | Eight. | Fifteen. |
| Two. | Nine. | Sixteen. |
| Three. | Ten. | Seventeen. |
| Four. | Eleven. | Eighteen. |
| Five. | Twelve. | Nineteen. |
| Six. | Thirteen. | Twenty. |

### Page 25, Vocabulary, Exercise C (Track 21)

A:    Hi, I'm Dmitry. My student ID number is zero seven, twelve, twenty. My email address is Dmitry K at zee mail dot com. My phone number is two nine oh four three four six.

### Page 25, Vocabulary, Exercise D (Track 22)

A:    Hi, I'm Amelia. My student ID number is zero four, eighteen, fourteen. My email address is Amelia eleven at link mail dot com. My phone number is three oh four, seven nine one four.

B:    Hi, I'm Max. My student ID number is zero six, fifteen, ten. My email address is Max nineteen at star link dot net. My phone number is six one five, six eight oh seven.

C:    Hi, I'm Leah. My student ID number is zero eight, eleven, seventeen. My email address is Leah Yu at C – C – F dot E-D-U. My phone number is five oh five, seven seven one two.

### Page 28, Speaking, Exercise B (Track 23)

A:    Hello?

B:    Hi, Leo.

A:    Uh, hi. Excuse me, who's calling?

B:    It's Max.

A:    Oh, hi Max! Sorry! Your phone number is different.

B:    Yeah, it's new. It's now six nine seven, eight oh seven five.

### Page 29, Speaking, Exercise E (Track 24)

*Conversation 1*

A:    Hello?

B:    Hi, Ryan.

A:    Uh, hi. Excuse me, who's calling?

B:    It's Tony.

A:    Oh, hi Tony! Sorry! Your phone number is different.

B:    Yeah. It's now seven oh two, one six three nine.

*Conversation 2*

A:    Hello?

B:    Hi, Sofia.

A:    Uh, hi. Excuse me, who's calling?

B:    It's Emma, your classmate.

A:    Oh, hi Emma! Your number isn't in my phone. Is it nine one six, eight oh seven seven?

B:    Yeah.

# UNIT 5
### Page 31, Vocabulary, Exercise A (Track 25)

*Places in a neighborhood*

1. ATM
2. bank
3. bus stop
4. cafe / coffee shop
5. gym
6. movie theater
7. park
8. post office
9. restaurant
10. school
11. store
12. supermarket

### Page 31, Vocabulary, Exercise D (Track 26)

*Conversation 1*

Maria:    Hello?

Emma:    Hi, Maria. It's Emma. Are you at school?

Maria:    No, I'm at home.

*Conversation 2*

Jon:      Hello?

Tomas:    Hey Jon; it's Tomas. We're at the restaurant.

Jon:      Sorry! I'm at the ATM.

*Conversation 3*

Marc:     Hello?

Bill:     Marc? Hey, it's Bill.

Marc:     Bill?

Bill:     Yeah, it's Bill from school. We're in the same English class.

Marc:     Oh yeah. Hi. I'm at a movie theater. I can't talk now.

## Page 33, Grammar, Exercises E and F (Track 27)

On High Street, there's a park.

There are some trees in the park.

There's a school.

There are two movie theaters.

There are some cars on the street.

There are no garages.

## Page 34, Speaking, Exercise B (Track 28)

A:   Excuse me?

B:   Yes?

A:   Is there an ATM around here?

B:   Yeah. Go straight and turn right on Jay Street. The ATM is on the left.

A:   Great, thanks!

## Page 35, Speaking, Exercise E (Track 29)

*Conversation 1*

A:   Excuse me? Is there a subway station around here?

B:   Yes. Turn right on Jay Street. The station is on the right.

*Conversation 2*

A:   Excuse me? Is there a supermarket around here?

B:   Yeah. Go straight. Then turn left on Main Street. There's a supermarket on the left.

*Conversation 3*

A:   Excuse me? Is there a bookstore around here?

B:   Yes. Go straight on Court. Then turn right on Main Street. The bookstore is on the left.

*Conversation 4*

A:   Excuse me? Is there a coffee shop around here?

B:   Um, yeah. Turn left on Jay Street and go straight. On Pine Street, turn right. There's a coffee shop on the right.

*Conversation 5*

A:   Excuse me? Is there a gas station around here?

B:   Yes. Turn left on Jay Street and go straight. On Pine turn right. The gas station is on the left.

*Conversation 6*

A:   Excuse me? Is there a post office around here?

B:   Yeah, there is.  Go straight on Court. Then turn left on Main Street and go straight. On Pine, turn right. The post office is on the left.

# UNIT 6

## Page 37, Vocabulary, Exercise A (Track 30)

1. China / Chinese
2. Japan / Japanese
3. Portugal / Portuguese
4. Vietnam / Vietnamese
5. Australia / Australian
6. Brazil / Brazilian
7. Peru / Peruvian
8. Canada / Canadian
9. Korea / Korean
10. Mexico / Mexican
11. The United States / American
12. Venezuela / Venezuelan
13. The United Kingdom / British
14. Spain / Spanish
15. Turkey / Turkish
16. Sweden / Swedish

## Page 37, Vocabulary, Exercise D (Track 31)

1. The 2020 Olympic Games are in Japan.
2. Canberra is a city in Australia.
3. English and French are the two main languages in Canada.
4. There are over a billion people in China.
5. Pho is the name of a Vietnamese soup.
6. Wales is a country in the United Kingdom.
7. Turkey is a country in both Europe and Asia.

8. Soccer player Cristiano Ronaldo is Portuguese.

9. This is the Peruvian flag.

10. Chichen Itza is in Mexico.

### Page 39, Grammar, Exercise F (Track 32)

1. There are two Mexican restaurants near here.

2. Venice is my favorite city.

3. Kimchee is a Korean food.

4. He's a famous actor.

### Page 40, Speaking, Exercise B (Track 33)

Mei: Where are you from, Luis?

Luis: The Dominican Republic. And you?

Mei: I'm from China.

Luis: Oh? Where in China?

Mei: Suzhou. It's a city near Shanghai. It's famous for its beautiful parks.

# PUT IT TOGETHER 2

### Page 42, Grammar, Exercise B (Track 34)

1. Is it a computer?

2. Are they in Lima?

3. Is she your friend?

4. What is it?

5. Where are they?

6. Who is she?

### Page 43, Grammar, Exercise F (Track 35)

Celia: Hey, Lynn. It's nice to see you. Who's your friend?

Lynn: Celia, this is Anong. She's our new classmate.

Celia: Hi, Anong. Where are you from?

Anong: I'm from Thailand.

Celia: Nice! Are you from Bangkok?

Anong: No, I'm not. I'm from a small city, Chiang Rai. Where are you from, Celia?

Celia: I'm from Brazil.

Anong: Where in Brazil?

Celia: From Sao Paulo.

Anong: Well, it's nice to meet you, Celia…Hey, is our class in Room 15?

Lynn: No, today it's in Room 10.

Anong: OK. Who's our teacher today?

Lynn: It's Ms. Lopez.

Anong: Got it. See you later then.

Celia & Lynn: Bye, Anong.

# UNIT 7

### Page 47, Vocabulary, Exercise A (Track 36)

1. grandmother

2. grandfather

3. mother (mom)

4. father (dad)

5. older sister

6. younger brother

7. aunt

8. uncle

9. cousin

10. grandparents

11. parents

### Page 48, Grammar, Exercise C (Track 37)

| | | |
|---|---|---|
| Twenty-one. | Thirty. | Thirty-nine. |
| Twenty-two. | Thirty-one. | Forty. |
| Twenty-three. | Thirty-two. | Fifty. |
| Twenty-four. | Thirty-three. | Sixty. |
| Twenty-five. | Thirty-four. | Seventy. |
| Twenty-six. | Thirty-five. | Eighty. |
| Twenty-seven. | Thirty-six. | Ninety. |
| Twenty-eight. | Thirty-seven. | One hundred. |
| Twenty-nine. | Thirty-eight. | |

### Page 49, Grammar, Exercise D (Track 38)

| | | |
|---|---|---|
| Twenty-two. | Fifty-nine. | Eighty-eight. |
| Thirty-six. | Sixty-four. | Ninety-seven. |
| Forty-five. | Seventy-one. | |

### Page 50, Speaking, Exercise B (Track 39)

Marie: That's a great photo of you.

Colin: Thanks.

Marie: And who's that? Your brother?

Colin: No. That's my cousin.

Marie: You look like him!

Colin:    Yeah, but he's younger.

Marie:    Oh? How old is he?

Colin:    He's nineteen.

## Page 51, Speaking, Exercise D (Track 40)

*Conversation 1*

A:    That's a great photo of you.

B:    Thanks.

A:    And who's that? Your mom?

B:    No. That's my aunt. She's only twenty-four.

A:    You look like her!

B:    Yeah. I know.

*Conversation 2*

A:    That's a great photo of you.

B:    Thanks.

A:    And who's that? Your dad?

B:    No. That's my grandfather.

A:    Really? How old is he?

B:    Seventy!

# UNIT 8

## Page 53, Vocabulary, Exercise A (Track 41)

1. funny

2. popular

3. sad

4. scary

5. dance

6. hip hop

7. pop

8. rock

## Page 53, Vocabulary, Exercise C (Track 42)

1. She's a Korean pop singer.

2. They're in a rock band.

3. He's a hip hop singer.

4. She listens to dance music.

5. It's a sad TV show.

6. It's a funny video.

7. It's a scary movie.

8. *Game of Thrones* is a popular TV show around the world.

## Page 54, Grammar, Exercise B    (*Page 43*)

1. Play video games

2. Watch movies

3. Read comic books

## Page 55, Grammar, Exercise D    (*Page 44*)

1. She plays video games.

2. He watches funny movies.

3. Ms. Davis reads long books.

4. Our teacher writes a lot.

## Page 56, Speaking, Exercise B (Track 45)

Matt:    What's on TV?

Ken:    Well, there's a soccer game.

Matt:    What else?

Ken:    *The Walking Dead* is on. Do you like that show?

Matt:    No, not really. It's scary. Do you like it?

Ken:    Yeah, I love it! It's my favorite show.

# UNIT 9

## Page 58, Vocabulary, Exercise A (Track 46)

1. It's three o'clock.

2. It's three oh five.
It's five after three.

3. It's three ten.
It's ten after three.

4. It's three fifteen.

5. It's three thirty.

6. It's three forty-five.
It's a quarter to four.

7. It's three fifty.
It's ten to four.

8. It's three fifty-five.
It's five to four.

## Page 59, Vocabulary, Exercise F (Track 47)

| *Classes* | Math | Break |
|-----------|---------|--------|
| English | Lunch | Art |
| Science | History | P.E. |

**Page 59, Vocabulary, Exercise G** (Track 48)

Hi, I'm Maya, and here's my class schedule for today.

English is at nine o'clock.

After English is science. It starts at nine fifty-five.

Then math is at ten fifty.

I eat lunch at noon, and then my history class is at one.

At one forty-five, I have a thirty-minute break.

And then my favorite class – art – is at two fifteen.

My last class is P.E. It starts at three ten.

**Page 60, Grammar, Exercise A** (Track 49)

1. morning
2. afternoon
3. evening
4. before
5. after
6. today
7. tomorrow

**Page 61, Grammar, Exercise F** (Track 50)

*Conversation 1*

A:     What time is your reservation?

B:     6:00.

A:     Are you all here now?

B:     Yes, we are.

A:     Please come with me.

*Conversation 2*

A:     When is your test?

B:     It's tomorrow.

A:     What time is it exactly?

B:     It's at 10:00 in the morning.

A:     Good luck!

*Conversation 3*

A:     When is swim practice?

B:     It's after school.

A:     Is it today?

B:     No, it's tomorrow at 4:00.

A:     Thanks.

**Page 61, Grammar, Exercise G** (Track 51)

*Conversation 1*

A:     What time is your reservation?

B:     6:00.

A:     Are you all here now?

B:     Yes, we are.

A:     Please come with me.

*Conversation 2*

A:     When is your test?

B:     It's tomorrow.

A:     What time is it exactly?

B:     It's at 10:00 in the morning.

A:     Good luck!

*Conversation 3*

A:     When is swim practice?

B:     It's after school.

A:     Is it today?

B:     No, it's tomorrow at 4:00.

A:     Thanks.

**Page 62, Speaking, Exercise B** (Track 52)

A:     Our big test is tomorrow.

B:     Yeah, I know. Let's study together.

A:     That sounds good. When?

B:     At 2:00?

A:     Sorry, I can't. I have class. Are you free later…at 3:30?

B:     Yeah. Let's meet then.

**Page 63, Speaking, Exercise F** (Track 53)

*Conversation 1*

A:     Let's see the new Batman movie today.

B:     I can't. I have a lot of homework.

A:     Are you free tomorrow?

B:     Yeah, in the afternoon.

A:     Great. There's a movie at 2:45.

B:     OK, let's see it then.

A:     That sounds good!

*Conversation 2*

A:     I need new shoes.

B:     Me too. Let's go shopping after school.

A:     Sorry, I can't. I have soccer practice.

B:     Are you free later?

A:     Yeah, at 5:30.

B:     Let's go shopping then.

A:     Sounds good!

# PUT IT TOGETHER 3

**Page 65, Grammar, Exercise F (Track 54)**

1. Question: Do I know you?

Answer: Yes, you do.

2. Question: Do they play video games?

Answer: Yes, they do.

3. Question: Does the store open at 10:00?

Answer: No, it doesn't.

**Page 66, See It and Say It, Exercise C (Track 55)**

*Conversation A*

A: What time is it?

B: It's 8:00.

A: Oh, good. *The Voice* is on.

B: I don't know it.

A: It's a show with singers. Watch.

B: Wow! He's really good!

A: Yeah, and he's only 16.

*Conversation B*

A: Do you like video games?

B: (tween, male) Yes, I do. This one is my favorite. It's scary.

A: Is it difficult?

B: No, not really. Let's play it!

*Conversation C*

A: What time is *Family Guy* on?

B: At 8:30.

A: Great! It's 8:00 now.

B: I don't like *Family Guy*. It's boring.

A: I love it! It's funny!

# UNIT 10

**Page 68, Vocabulary, Exercise A (Track 56)**

1. get up

2. take a shower

3. get dressed

4. go to school

5. start school

6. finish school

7. go home

8. do homework

9. go to bed

**Page 71, Grammar, Exercise H (Track 57)**

1. It's the first day of school.

2. The night before, I often choose my clothes.

3. I usually check my backpack.

4. Sometimes I go to bed early.

5. I am never nervous.

6. On the first day of school, I get up late sometimes.

7. I always take a shower.

8. I usually go to school early.

9. I am always excited.

**Page 72, Speaking, Exercise C (Track 58)**

Bill: I'm so happy it's Friday! I need a break.

Nadia: Yeah, me too. What do you usually do on the weekend, Bill?

Bill: Not much. I get up late. Sometimes, I see my friends. What about you?

Nadia: Oh, I'm really busy. I have a class on Saturday morning. Then I work on Saturday afternoon. On Sunday, I do homework.

Bill: Wow, you *are* busy!

# UNIT 11

**Page 74, Vocabulary, Exercise A (Track 59)**

| | | |
|---|---|---|
| January | May | September |
| February | June | October |
| March | July | November |
| April | August | December |

**Page 75, Vocabulary, Exercise E (Track 60)**

| | | |
|---|---|---|
| first | eleventh | twenty-first |
| second | twelfth | twenty-second |
| third | thirteenth | twenty-third |
| fourth | fourteenth | twenty-fourth |
| fifth | fifteenth | twenty-fifth |
| sixth | sixteenth | twenty-sixth |
| seventh | seventeenth | twenty-seventh |
| eighth | eighteenth | twenty-eighth |
| ninth | nineteenth | twenty-ninth |
| tenth | twentieth | thirtieth |

### Page 75, Vocabulary, Exercise F (Track 61)

1. Today is July fourth.
2. Today is March second.
3. Today is May first.
4. Today is October eleventh.
5. Today is September third.
6. Today is August twenty-fifth.
7. Today is January thirty-first.
8. Today is April thirteenth.
9. Today is February twenty-second.
10. Today is November sixteenth.
11. Today is June thirtieth.
12. Today is December tenth.

### Page 76, Grammar, Exercise D (Track 62)

Dai: Good morning. I'm Dai. Dai Suzuki.

Woman: Good morning, Dai. Hmm OK, I see your name. You're checked in.

Dai: Thanks. Where does the class meet?

Woman: You're in Room 11.

Dai: OK. How do I get there?

Woman: Go straight down the hall and turn right. It's the second door on your left.

Dai: Great. When does the class start?

Woman: Let's see…in about ten minutes.

Dai: Oh, and what time does it finish?

Woman: At 9:15.

Dai: Thanks a lot.

### Page 78, Speaking, Exercise C (Track 63)

Zac: When is the school Halloween party—Friday or Saturday?

Carlos: I'm not sure. Check online.

Zac: OK. Um, it's on Saturday, the thirtieth.

Carlos: What time does it start?

Zac: At 9:00. Let's go.

Carlos: Sounds good!

# UNIT 12
### Page 80, Vocabulary, Exercise A (Track 64)

1. steak and fries
2. tea
3. cereal and fruit, coffee, orange juice
4. soup and salad with bread
5. pizza
6. chicken and rice
7. ice cream
8. pasta

### Page 81, Vocabulary, Exercise B (Track 65)

1. steak and fries
2. cereal and fruit
3. soup and salad
4. chicken and rice

### Page 81, Vocabulary, Exercise D (Track 66)

1. Today's breakfast is cereal with fruit and orange juice. But first, I need my coffee.

2. Look! It's my favorite dinner … pasta!

3. It's pizza again for lunch…my third time this week! I know, I know…I eat a lot of pizza, but it's SO good!

4. I'm at Café Fes. The Moroccan mint tea here is delicious!

5. Dinner tonight is chicken and rice from the restaurant near school. Yum!

6. And now, it's time for dessert! Mmmm…this ice cream is *really* good.

7. The steak at this restaurant is delicious. The fries are good, too.

8. Just a light lunch for me today: my mom's homemade soup and a salad. Oh, and some good bread!

### Page 81, Vocabulary, Exercise E (Track 67)

1. Today's breakfast is cereal with fruit and orange juice. But first, I need my coffee.

2. Look! It's my favorite dinner … pasta!

3. It's pizza again for lunch…my third time this week! I know, I know…I eat a lot of pizza, but it's SO good!

4. I'm at Café Fes. The Moroccan mint tea here is delicious!

5. Dinner tonight is chicken and rice from the restaurant near school. Yum!

6. And now, it's time for dessert! Mmmm…this ice cream is *really* good.

7. The steak at this restaurant is delicious. The fries are good, too.

8. Just a light lunch for me today: my mom's homemade soup and a salad. Oh, and some good bread!

## Page 82, Grammar, Exercsie A (Track 68)

1. a bowl of rice
2. a cup of coffee
3. a slice of toast
4. a glass of water
5. a piece of cake
6. a bag of chips

## Page 83, Grammar, Exercise F (Track 69)

Will: Mom, can I have a snack?

Mom: Will, it's 4:30 now. Dinner is in an hour.

Will: But, Mom, I'm hungry!

Mom: OK. Do you want a piece of fruit? We have some oranges.

Will: No, I want some ice cream.

Mom: No, Will, that's for dessert.

Will: OK, can I have some chips?

Mom: No, that's not healthy. Eat a small bowl of soup, or drink a glass of juice.

Will: OK.

## Page 84, Speaking, Exercise C (Track 70)

Server: Who's next?

Paula: Hi, I'd like the chicken sandwich, please.

Server: Anything else?

Paula: Yeah, a bottle of water and a bag of chips.

Server: OK. The chicken sandwich, a bottle of water, and a bag of chips. That's $6.50.

Paula: Here you go.

Server: Thanks. And here's your food.

# PUT IT TOGETHER 4

## Page 89, What Do You Usually Do on Your Birthday?, Exercise B (Track 71)

*Narrator: Conversation 1*

A: What do you usually do on your birthday?

B: I usually have a big party. But not this year.

A: Why is that?

B: My birthday is on Monday this year. It's not a good day for a party.

*Narrator: Conversation 2*

A: What do you usually do on your birthday?

B: I eat dinner with my family at home.

A: What do you eat?

B: My mom makes steaks, and we have ice cream for dessert!

## UNIT 1
(Track 72)

answer (the question)
ask (your teacher)
circle (the word)
close (your book)
cover (the page)
listen (and repeat)

look at (the picture)
open (your book)
read (the sentence)
say (the word)
write (your name)

**Word Bank**

yes
no

please
numbers 1–5

**Grammar**

Listen to the conversation.      Open your books.

**Speaking**

Good morning
/ afternoon / evening.

Can you repeat that? / Can you say that again?

## UNIT 2
(Track 73)

A B C D E F G H I J K L M N O P Q R S T U V W X Y Z

businessman/woman
doctor
programmer
soccer player
student
teacher

**Word Bank**

Mr. / Ms.

**Grammar**

I'm a student.      You're a student.      She's a teacher.

**Speaking**

Hello. / Hi.
I'm Aya. / My name is Aya.
(It's) nice to meet you (too).

## UNIT 3
(Track 74)

A B C D E F G H I J K L M N O P Q R S T U V W X Y Z

businessman/woman
doctor
programmer
soccer player
student
teacher

**Word Bank**

Mr. / Ms.

**Grammar**

I'm a student.
You're a student.
She's a teacher.

**Speaking**

Hello. / Hi.
I'm Aya. / My name is Aya.
(It's) nice to meet you (too).

## PUT IT TOGETHER 1
(Track 75)

**Word Bank**

I don't know.

**Grammar**

Am I in this class? / Yes, you are. No, you're not.
Are you a student? / Yes, I am. No, I'm not.
Is she a teacher? / Yes, she is. No, she's not.
Are they students? / Yes, they are. No, they're not.

## UNIT 4
(Track 76)

| | | |
|---|---|---|
| zero | seven | fourteen |
| one | eight | fifteen |
| two | nine | sixteen |
| three | ten | seventeen |
| four | eleven | eighteen |
| five | twelve | nineteen |
| six | thirteen | twenty |

student ID number
email address

phone number
What's your email address / phone number?
   It's…

**Word Bank**

| | | |
|---|---|---|
| @ = at | .net = dot net | new |
| .com = dot com | (best) friend | Sorry! |
| .edu = dot e-d-u | different | Yeah. |

## Grammar

Your ID number is 16.

Her phone number is 555–2436.

Its name is Maru.

This is our class.

## Speaking

Hello?

Hi, it's Max.

Excuse me, who's calling?

# UNIT 5
(Track 77)

| | | |
|---|---|---|
| ATM | park | neighborhood |
| bank | post office | car |
| bus stop | restaurant | garage |
| cafe / coffee shop | school | tree |
| gym | store | |
| movie theater | supermarket | |

## Word Bank

| | | |
|---|---|---|
| Word Bank | clothing store | favorite |
| bookstore | department store | street |

## Grammar

There's an ATM on my street.

There are no / two / some stores in my neighborhood.

## Speaking

Excuse me. Is there a gym near here?

Go straight. Turn left / right on Jay Street.

Sorry, I don't know.

# UNIT 6
(Track 78)

| | |
|---|---|
| neighborhood | the United Kingdom / British |
| Australia / Australian | |
| Brazil / Brazilian | the United States / American |
| Canada / Canadian | Turkey / Turkish |
| China / Chinese | Venezuela / Venezuelan |
| Japan / Japanese | Vietnam / Vietnamese |
| Korea / Korean | in (+ city / country) |
| Mexico / Mexican | beautiful |
| Peru / Peruvian | big |
| Portugal / Portuguese | exciting |
| Spain / Spanish | old |
| Sweden / Swedish | small |

## Word Bank

| | | |
|---|---|---|
| flag | actor | interesting |
| French | famous | near |
| language | food | |
| soup | fun | |

## Grammar

New York is interesting.

New York is an interesting city.

## Speaking

Where are you from?

  (I'm from) China.

Where in China?

  Suzhou. It's near Shanghai.

My city is famous for its parks. / New York City is famous for Central Park.

# PUT IT TOGETHER 2
(Track 79)

## Word Bank

flight

job

## Grammar

Who is she? / (She's) my friend.

What is it? / (It's) a computer.

Where are they? / (They're) in Lima.

# UNIT 7
(Track 80)

| | | |
|---|---|---|
| mother (mom) | Twenty-one. | Thirty-four. |
| father (dad) | Twenty-two. | Thirty-five. |
| (older / younger) | Twenty-three. | Thirty-six. |
| sister | Twenty-four. | Thirty-seven. |
| (older / younger) | Twenty-five. | Thirty-eight. |
| brother | Twenty-six. | Thirty-nine. |
| grandmother | Twenty-seven. | Forty. |
| grandfather | Twenty-eight. | Fifty. |
| aunt | Twenty-nine. | Sixty. |
| uncle | Thirty. | Seventy. |
| cousin | Thirty-one. | Eighty. |
| parents | Thirty-two. | Ninety. |
| grandparents | Thirty-three. | One hundred |

## Word Bank

| | | |
|---|---|---|
| a lot of | (have) homework | on vacation |
| free time | husband | wife |

## Grammar

I have a big family.

He has short hair.

We have a lot of friends.

## Speaking

You look like your sister. / You look like her.

How old are you?

   I'm 19.

# UNIT 8

(Track 81)

| | |
|---|---|
| funny | pop |
| popular | rock |
| sad | play video games |
| scary | read comic books |
| dance | watch movies |
| hip hop | |

## Word Bank

| | |
|---|---|
| band/group | singer |
| club | song |

## Grammar

I like / She likes hip hop.

I don't like / She doesn't like hip hop.

## Speaking

Do you like rock?

   Yes, I love it!

/ Yeah, it's OK. / No, not really.

# UNIT 9

(Track 82)

What time is it?

   It's three o'clock.

/ It's three oh five. / It's three ten.

   It's three fifteen.

/ It's three thirty.

   It's three forty-five.

/ It's three fifty. / It's three fifty-five.

noon

midnight

at (+ time)

computer club

drama club

English club

swim practice

band practice

have an appointment

have a test

have class / swim practice

## Word Bank

| | | |
|---|---|---|
| art | science | test |
| history | lunch | go shopping |
| math | break | shoes |
| P.E. | reservation | |

## Grammar

When is English class?

It's at 2:00.

It's in the morning / afternoon / evening.

It's before / after math.

It's now / later / today / tomorrow.

## Speaking

Let's go shopping.

   (That) sounds great. / (Sorry,)

I can't. I have class.

Are you free at 2:00 / later / in the morning?

   Yes. / Yeah. / No. I have class.

# PUT IT TOGETHER 3

(Track 83)

## Word Bank

| | |
|---|---|
| pet | homeroom |
| difficult | invite |

## Grammar

Do you like math? / Yes, I do. No, I don't.

Does he read comic books? / Yes, he does. No, he doesn't.

Do they have homework? / Yes, they do. No, they don't.

# UNIT 10

(Track 84)

| | | |
|---|---|---|
| get up | do homework | Friday |
| take a shower | go to bed | Saturday |
| get dressed | Monday | Sunday |
| go to school | Tuesday | on (+ day of the week) |
| start/finish (school) | Wednesday | go (+ verb + ing) |
| go home | Thursday | go (+ to + place) |

## Word Bank

| | | |
|---|---|---|
| routine | early | miss (class) |
| choose | late | nervous |

## Grammar

He is always / usually
/ often / sometimes
/ never late.
She always / usually
/ often / sometimes
/ never gets up early.

## Speaking

What do you usually do on the weekend?
  Not much. I get up late. Sometimes I see my friends.
  I'm really busy. I have a class on Saturday morning.

# UNIT 11
(Track 85)

| | | |
|---|---|---|
| January | fourth | twentieth |
| February | fifth | twenty-first |
| March | sixth | twenty-second |
| April | seventh | twenty-third |
| May | eighth | twenty-fourth |
| June | ninth | twenty-fifth |
| July | tenth | twenty-sixth |
| August | eleventh | twenty-seventh |
| September | twelfth | twenty-eighth |
| October | thirteenth | twenty-ninth |
| November | fourteenth | thirtieth |
| December | fifteenth | thirty-first |
| first | sixteenth | in (+ month) |
| second | seventeenth | on (+ date) |
| third | eighteenth | by (+ bus / car) |
| | nineteenth | |

## Word Bank

| | |
|---|---|
| birthday | New Year's Day |
| What do you do? | New Year's Eve |
| have a party | film festival |
| check in | food festival |
| buy | last |
| serve | Seasons of the year |
| wear | |

## Grammar

Where do you live? / (I live) in Santiago.
When do they study? / (They study) in April.
How does she go to school? (She goes to school) by bus.

## Speaking

When is the Halloween party?
  It's this Saturday.
  I'm not sure. Is it on Saturday?
  I don't know. / I have no idea.

# UNIT 12
(Track 86)

| | | |
|---|---|---|
| bread | orange juice | tea |
| cereal | pasta | bread |
| chicken | pizza | cake |
| coffee | rice | chips |
| fries | salad | pie |
| fruit | soup | popcorn |
| ice cream | steak | |

## Word Bank

| | | |
|---|---|---|
| breakfast / lunch / dinner | milk | healthy |
| | soda | hungry |
| dessert | water | snack |
| eat | delicious | |
| drink | good | |

## Grammar

I want some rice.
I want a bowl of rice / a cup of coffee / a slice of bread.
I want a glass of water / a piece of cake / a bag of chips.

## Speaking

I'd like the chicken sandwich, (please).
Anything else?
  A bag of chips, (please). / No thanks.
That's $6.50.
  Here you go.

# PUT IT TOGETHER 4
(Track 87)

## Word Bank

dish

## Grammar

Are you Peruvian? / Yes, I am. No, I'm not.
Where are you from? / (I'm from) Peru.
Do you live in Tokyo? / Yes, I do. No, I'm don't.
Where do you live exactly? / (I live in) Nezu.